Contents

Part 1

Part 2

i

Circle the word that names the picture. Then write the word.

b<u>e</u>d

1.  cheek (check) cook *check*	**2.** bull ball bell	**3.** sled slide slap
4. step stamp stop	**5.** ten tan tone	**6.** bag bug beg
7. boat belt bite	**8.** pet pat pot	**9.** pine pan pen
10. nut nest net	**11.** men man mane	**12.** shall shell school

Name _____

Below are eight riddles. The answers are in the box. Write each answer on the correct line.

an egg	You can spend both of them.
red pepper	an elephant on roller skates
"Hello, hello!"	They have no cents.
a bed	a ten-cent coin

1. What is very big and has 16 wheels?

an elephant on roller skates

2. What has four legs and only one foot?

_____

3. What stays hot even when it gets cold?

_____

4. What has a head and tail but no body?

_____

5. What do you say to a monster with two heads?

_____

6. What goes up white and comes down white and yellow?

_____

7. How is time like money?

_____

8. Why are silly people like people without money?

_____

Phonics Home Activity: Ask your child to circle the words in which he or she hears the short *e* sound. Then have your child make up riddles using as many of the words as possible.

Circle the word that names each picture. Then write the word.

s_i_x **6**

1.	pot	plug	(pig)	*pig*
2.	chin	chime	chain	
3.	swan	swing	sway	
4.	bib	but	baby	
5.	grief	gift	gave	
6.	ring	rang	rung	
7.	crab	cub	crib	
8.	brads	bridge	braids	
9.	shape	shop	ship	
10.	laps	lops	lips	

Name _____

Write the word from the box that completes each sentence.

grin	drill	rinse	twig
rid	spill	lit	quit

1. Please don't _____*quit*_____ until you finish your work.

2. Hold the glass carefully or the water may _____.

3. How will we get _____ of all the leaves that fell in our yard?

4. Father _____ the fire with a match.

5. I broke a little _____ off the bush.

6. John has a happy _____ on his face.

7. Father used a _____ to make a hole in the wood.

8. I will wash and _____ the spoons.

Now use the words you just wrote in this puzzle.
Print each word next to the number of its sentence.

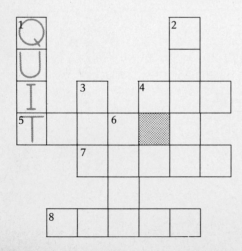

Phonics Home Activity: Ask your child to copy the words in the box at the top of the page and to circle the vowel in each one. Then help your child to look in a newspaper or magazine to find and cut out words that contain the short *i* sound.

Say each picture name. Write **short o** if the picture name has the short *o* sound.

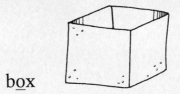

b<u>o</u>x

1. *short o*	**2.** ___	**3.** ___	**4.** ___
5. ___	**6.** ___	**7.** ___	**8.** ___
9. ___	**10.** ___	**11.** ___	**12.** ___
13. ___	**14.** ___	**15.** ___	**16.** ___

Name ___

Find the word in the box that goes with each clue.
Print the word.

flock	plot	pods	socks
shock	jog	blond	clog

1. to run slowly j o g
                         8

2. to surprise or upset ____ ____ ____ ____ ____
                                 7   5

3. what happens in a story ____ ____ ____ ____
                                        3

4. a hair color ____ ____ ____ ____ ____
                        2

5. for the feet ____ ____ ____ ____ ____
                                        6

6. a group of birds ____ ____ ____ ____
                                 1

7. to become blocked up ____ ____ ____ ____
                                4

8. what peas grow in ____ ____ ____
                            9

Now complete the riddle. Print the letter that you
wrote above each number in the space with the
same number.

Where would you never run out of time?

In a ____ ____ ____ ____ ____ ____ ____ ____ ____
      1   2   3   4   5   6   7   8   9

---

8 **Phonics Home Activity:** Ask your child to read each clue and the answer he or she wrote. Then have
your child read the completed riddle. Take turns with your child trying to make up riddles that have two
word answers in which each word has a short *o* sound.

Say each picture name. The name is hiding in the letters. Find the word and circle it. Then write the word.

1. sr(pump)et

pump

2. replugeg

3. cupigr

4. dubudkd

5. trsudsme

6. brushure

7. tricuff

8. egrug

9. deebulb

10. trunkmet

11. tidrumy

12. teskunkul

Name _____

9

Read each sentence. Circle the picture that goes with it. Then write the underlined word.

1. That boot has <u>mud</u> on it.

mud

2. She will <u>scrub</u> the dog.

_____

3. He has a <u>bunch</u> of flowers.

_____

4. I will have good <u>luck</u>.

_____

5. This has <u>dust</u> on it.

_____

6. That big boat has <u>sunk</u>.

_____

7. What a <u>plump</u> little cat!

_____

Phonics Home Activity: Ask your child to read each sentence and point to the picture he or she chose. Then, on another sheet of paper, have your child write and illustrate an original sentence that contains one of the underlined words.

Say each picture name. Fill in the circle next to the word that names the picture.

★	○ bunk ● bank ○ bake	1.	○ stunts ○ starts ○ stilts	2.	○ wide ○ web ○ wage
3.	○ trunk ○ trick ○ track	4.	○ cluck ○ clock ○ click	5.	○ brick ○ brush ○ breath
6.	○ drill ○ dull ○ dried	7.	○ bench ○ break ○ branch	8.	○ date ○ dust ○ dots
9.	○ steam ○ stem ○ stun	10.	○ drop ○ drum ○ dime	11.	○ wig ○ wag ○ web
12.	○ van ○ vine ○ vane	13.	○ brake ○ brick ○ brook	14.	○ cot ○ cat ○ cut

©

Number right _____

Name _____

11

check

Fill in the circle next to the word that completes each sentence.

★ I put a _____ on my flat tire.
○ pitch   ● patch   ○ peach

1. This _____ will hold the papers together.
○ clap   ○ coop   ○ clip

2. Will you _____ me your pencil?
○ land   ○ lend   ○ load

3. This _____ will keep my dress clean.
○ smock   ○ smack   ○ smoke

4. I must _____, or I will be late.
○ rash   ○ reach   ○ rush

5. That glass has a big _____ in it.
○ creak   ○ crack   ○ croak

6. My brother and I have _____ hair.
○ blond   ○ blind   ○ blend

7. Now I will do a magic _____!
○ truck   ○ track   ○ trick

8. Look at that big _____ of birds.
○ flock   ○ flick   ○ flake

Number right _____ ©

12 **Phonics Home Activity:** Ask your child to read the sentences that she or he has completed. Then have your child circle the letters that stand for the vowel sound in each answer word.

Circle the word that names each picture. Then write **long a** if the word has the long *a* sound.

v<u>a</u>s<u>e</u>

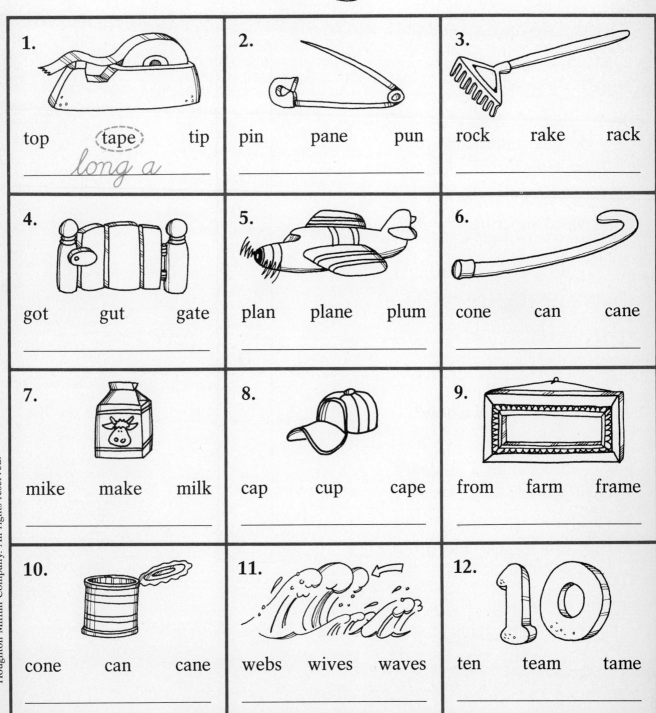

1.
top (tape) tip
long a

2.
pin pane pun
_____

3.
rock rake rack
_____

4.
got gut gate
_____

5.
plan plane plum
_____

6.
cone can cane
_____

7.
mike make milk
_____

8.
cap cup cape
_____

9.
from farm frame
_____

10.
cone can cane
_____

11.
webs wives waves
_____

12.
ten team tame
_____

Name _____

Find the word in the box that answers each question. Then print the word. Put one letter in each space.

pane	chase	paste	shave
tame	blade	grade	

1. What word means "glue"? P A S T E

2. How do men take hair off their faces? ___ ___ ___ ___ ___

3. What word describes a pet? ___ ___ ___ ___

4. Which part of a knife is sharp? ___ ___ ___ ___ ___

   O

5. What is part of a window? ___ ___ ___ ___

6. What word names a student's level in school? ___ ___ ___ ___ ___

7. What word means "run after"? ___ ___ ___ ___ ___

Now look at the letters in the black box. If you got all the answers right, those letters will tell you something that is in each of your answer words. What is it?

___ ___ ___ **O** ___ ___ ___ !

Phonics Home Activity: Help your child to list other words that contain the long *a* sound. Then play "The Name Game." Point out that the words *name* and *game* contain the long *a* sound. Help your child list as many names as possible that also contain the long *a* sound. Examples include James, Jane, Kate, Jake, and Gail.

Circle the word that names the picture. Then write the word.

j<u>ee</u>p

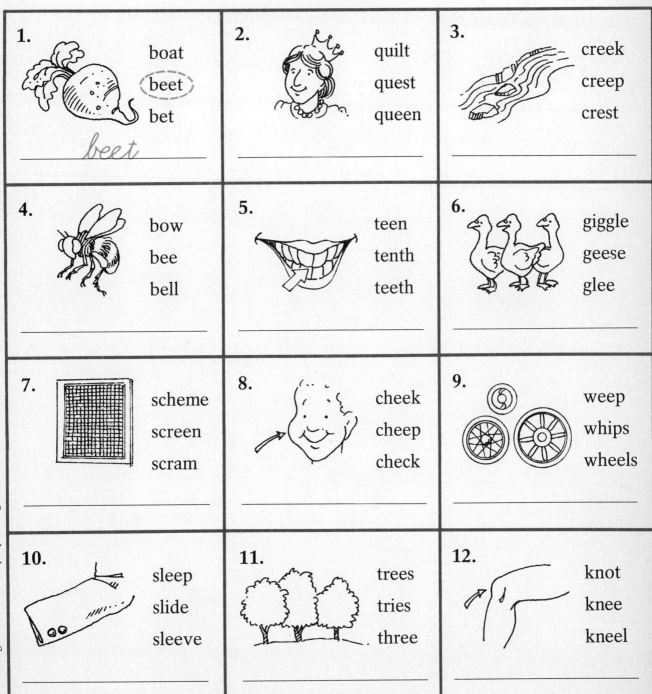

1.
boat
(beet)
bet

beet

2.
quilt
quest
queen

3.
creek
creep
crest

4.
bow
bee
bell

5.
teen
tenth
teeth

6.
giggle
geese
glee

7.
scheme
screen
scram

8.
cheek
cheep
check

9.
weep
whips
wheels

10.
sleep
slide
sleeve

11.
trees
tries
three

12.
knot
knee
kneel

Name _____

Read each sentence. Circle the picture that goes with it. Then write the underlined word.

1. Mom put up the <u>screen</u>.

screen

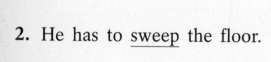

2. He has to <u>sweep</u> the floor.

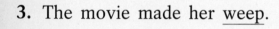

3. The movie made her <u>weep</u>.

4. Tim <u>squeezed</u> his puppy.

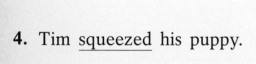

5. Ana will <u>weed</u> the garden.

16 **Phonics Home Activity:** Ask your child to read each sentence on the page, point to the correct picture and explain why the other two pictures are not correct. Then, on a separate sheet of paper, have your child write new sentences for two of the underlined words and then illustrate them.

Write a word to complete each sentence.

k<u>i</u>t<u>e</u>

ripe   **file**   **dime**

This fruit is beautiful and
one costs only a ___*dime*___.
It is _____, so it
will taste good.

twine   **white**   **bride**

The _____ is my sister.
She made her own dress out of
_____ cloth.

chime   **crime**   **strike**

This sounds like a bell.
It is a _____, though.
I will _____ it with a
little hammer.

pride   **slide**   **twice**

Let's take turns.
You go down the _____ two
times. Then I will go down
_____.

Name _____

Find the word in the box that goes with each clue.
Write the word.

hikes	stripe	spine	crime
wise	spice	strikes	whine

1. hits very hard _____*strikes*_____

2. very long walks _____

3. part of your back _____

4. what police are against _____

5. line of color _____

6. very smart _____

7. a small sad noise _____

8. something you put into food _____

Now find each word you just wrote in this puzzle.
Draw a line around each word. The words go →
and ↓ .

```
W  I  S  E  N  I  N  E
S  Z  T  I  M  E  P  K
S  T  R  I  P  E  C  B
W  H  I  N  E  O  R  S
H  I  K  E  S  M  I  P
I  R  E  T  T  I  M  I
D  L  S  P  I  C  E  N
E  P  R  I  Z  E  S  E
```

18 **Phonics Home Activity:** Ask your child to read aloud each word that she or he found. Then have him or her hunt for the following words: *mice, prizes, hide, time, nine*.

Say each picture name. Write **long o** if the picture name has the long *o* sound.

r<u>o</u>p<u>e</u>

1. long o

2. _____

3. _____

4. _____

5. _____

6. _____

7. _____

8. _____

9. _____

10. _____

11. _____

12. _____

13. _____

14. _____

15. _____

16. _____

Name _____

Read this story. Then follow the directions below it.

One day Ann got a note in the mail from her friend Pat. She opened it, but she could not read it. She could read each word, but the message made no sense. It said: "I come hope to you my can party."

Ann called Pat on the phone. "I got your note," she said. "Is this a joke?"

Pat laughed. "No, silly," she said. "I wrote the message in code. To read it, draw a line around every other word. Read those words in order and then go back and read the other words. Call me when you have read the whole message."

Ann did what Pat said. Then she called Pat again. "I broke the code!" she said. "Yes, I can come to your party. Thank you for asking me, and thank you for teaching me that code."

Circle the word that completes each sentence. Then write the word.

1. Ann got a _____*note*_____ in the mail.

   wrote   (note)   hope

2. She asked, "Is this a _____?"

   code   note   joke

3. Pat wrote the message in _____.

   phone   note   code

4. The real message was: "I _____ you can come to my party."

   hope   whole   broke

Phonics Home Activity: Ask your child to circle the words in which they hear the long *o* sound. Then, on a separate sheet of paper, have your child write a message using the code described in this story.

Circle the word that names each picture. Then write the word.

m<u>u</u>le

1. under (uniform) uphill _uniform_

2. cone cub cube _____

3. bugle buggy bagel _____

4. tube table tub _____

5. glum glue glow _____

6. shot shut shoe _____

7. site suit sate _____

8. flutter flit flute _____

9. ruler roller railing _____

10. freight fruit fret _____

Name _____

long u

Each sentence tells about a word with the long *u* sound. The word is hiding in the letters. Find the word and circle it. Then print the word.

1. This is a drink made from fruit.

sa(juice)je   j u i c e

2. This word describes songs and other pretty sounds.

b m m u s i c t a _____

3. This word means a painful spot that a person might get after falling down.

b r i b r u i s e s t e _____

4. This word is another name for every person.

e i t t h u m a n k i _____

5. These two words name our country.

U n i t e d S t a t e s r e t e a s

_____

Phonics Home Activity: Ask your child to copy the answer words and to circle the letter that stands for the long *u* sound in each one. Then scramble these long *u* words and have your child unscramble them: *huge, cute, suit, shoe, truth, blue.*

Say each picture name. Fill in the circle next to the word that names the picture.

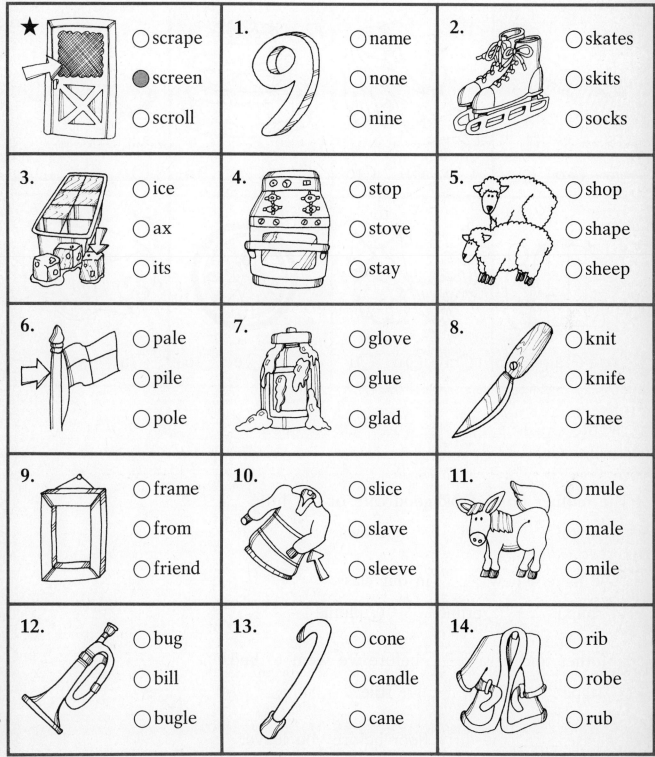

★
○ scrape
● screen
○ scroll

1.
○ name
○ none
○ nine

2.
○ skates
○ skits
○ socks

3.
○ ice
○ ax
○ its

4.
○ stop
○ stove
○ stay

5.
○ shop
○ shape
○ sheep

6.
○ pale
○ pile
○ pole

7.
○ glove
○ glue
○ glad

8.
○ knit
○ knife
○ knee

9.
○ frame
○ from
○ friend

10.
○ slice
○ slave
○ sleeve

11.
○ mule
○ male
○ mile

12.
○ bug
○ bill
○ bugle

13.
○ cone
○ candle
○ cane

14.
○ rib
○ robe
○ rub

©

Number right _____

Name _____

23

check

Say each picture name. Fill in the circle next to the vowel letter that stands for the long vowel sound in the word.

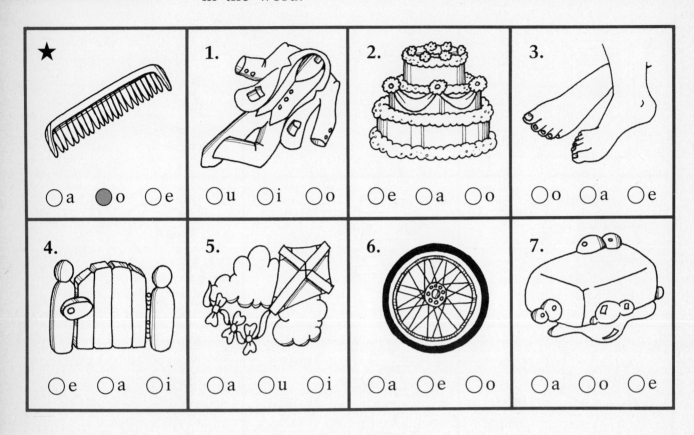

★
○ a ● o ○ e

1.
○ u ○ i ○ o

2.
○ e ○ a ○ o

3.
○ o ○ a ○ e

4.
○ e ○ a ○ i

5.
○ a ○ u ○ i

6.
○ a ○ e ○ o

7.
○ a ○ o ○ e

Fill in the circle next to the word that completes each sentence.

★ The mother horse took good care of her little _____ .

　○ choke 　● colt 　○ crows

8. We have a new _____ in our class.

　○ pupil 　○ prune 　○ plume

9. Mother told us a _____ before we went to bed.

　○ tape 　○ tale 　○ tile

10. Please _____ the dirty floor before you leave.

　○ sleep 　○ sweet 　○ sweep

Number right _____

Phonics Home Activity: Ask your child to name each picture at the top of the page and to tell what long vowel sound is heard in each picture name. Then have your child read the completed sentences and choose two of them to copy and illustrate on a separate sheet of paper.

Say each picture name. Write **long a** if the picture name has the long *a* sound. Write **short a** if the picture name has the short *a* sound.

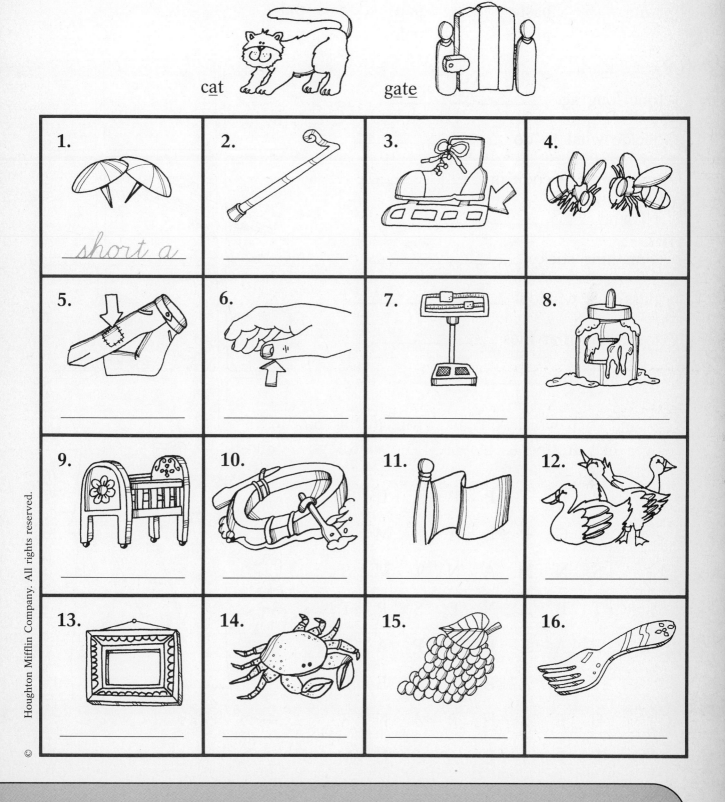

cat   gate

1. short a

2.

3.

4.

5.

6.

7.

8.

9.

10.

11.

12.

13.

14.

15.

16.

Name _____   **25**

Find the word in the box that goes with each clue.
Write the word.

plan	paste	pan	pal
pane	plane	pale	past

1. time long ago ___*past*___

2. decide what to do _____

3. something to cook in _____

4. a friend _____

5. something sticky _____

6. glass in a window _____

7. something that flies _____

8. light in color _____

Now find each word you just wrote in this puzzle.
Draw a line around each word. The words go → and ↓ .

```
P  L  T  P  P  A  L  P
A  G  P  L  A  N  M  A
S  N  M  A  N  T  M  S
T  B  A  N  E  S  P  T
P  A  L  E  A  P  A  E
T  G  A  E  L  A  E  E
H  E  S  H  P  A  N  S
E  P  T  L  A  G  H  M
```

Phonics Home Activity: Ask your child to read aloud each word that she or he found. If children enjoy the activity, have them hunt for additional words. (man, ants, bag, age, last, the, he)

Say each picture name. The name is hiding in the letters. Find the word and circle it. Then write the word.

b_ed   j_ee_p

1. tat**eeth**ng

   teeth

2. estanchef

   _____

3. sweeptdjk

   _____

4. trcheckmen

   _____

5. usecheekte

   _____

6. krshellder

   _____

7. kcpeelzr

   _____

8. grebeltee

   _____

9. geeseous

   _____

10. ewebily

    _____

11. rebeetst

    _____

12. qucentip

    _____

Name _____

Read this story. Write the word from the box that belongs in each space.

greet	best	teeth	stretched	swell
sleeve	screen	agreed	belt	creek

Harry could hear a bee buzzing against the window _____*screen*_____. Quickly, Harry jumped out of bed. He yawned, and he _____.

"What a wonderful day!" Harry said. "Today I will meet the queen! I must look my _____."

Harry brushed his _____ and washed his face. He put on his shirt with red dots and his new red pants. Then Harry buckled his shiny silver _____. Suddenly Harry cried, "Oh, no, I can't find my left shoe. What will I do?"

Harry felt something tugging at his shirt _____. It was his pet dog Rolf. Rolf had been swimming in the _____. He had taken Harry's shoe for a swim too. It was very wet.

"Oh, no," Harry said. "Now what will I do?" Rolf sniffed under Harry's bed and barked at Harry's fluffy red slippers. "Well, the queen's favorite color *is* red," Harry _____. So Harry went to _____ the queen in his bright red fluffy slippers. Harry looked _____!

Phonics Home Activity: Ask your child to read the completed story. Then ask your child to circle the words in which he or she hears the short *e* sound with a red crayon and the words with the long *e* sound with a green crayon.

Circle the word that names the picture. Then write the word.

pi_g   ki_t_e

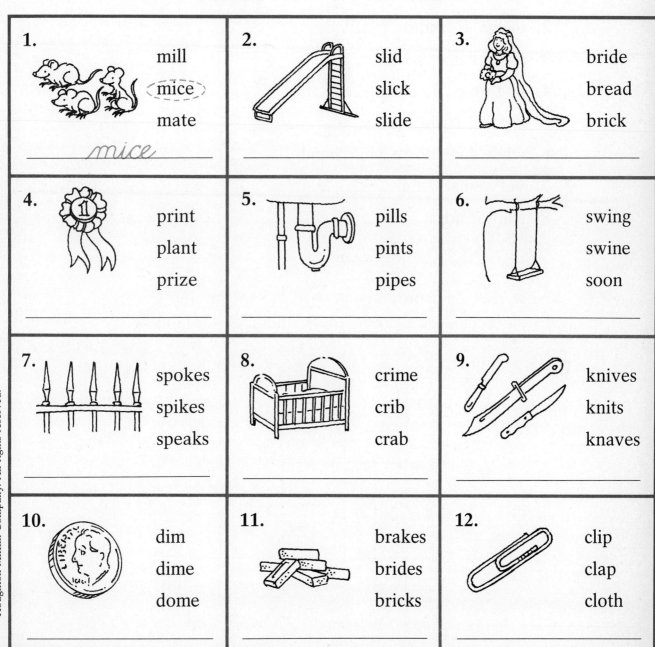

1.
mill
(mice)
mate

mice

2.
slid
slick
slide

3.
bride
bread
brick

4.
print
plant
prize

5.
pills
pints
pipes

6.
swing
swine
soon

7.
spokes
spikes
speaks

8.
crime
crib
crab

9.
knives
knits
knaves

10.
dim
dime
dome

11.
brakes
brides
bricks

12.
clip
clap
cloth

Name _____

Find the word in the box that goes with each clue.
Write the word.

spike	twine	chill	wise
lick	pitch	ripe	whine

1. how fruit should be _____ *ripe* _____

2. to make colder _____

3. a big nail _____

4. to throw _____

5. kind of string _____

6. what dogs do to your hand _____

7. very smart _____

8. a little noise _____

Now use the words you just wrote in this puzzle.
Print each word next to the number of the clue.

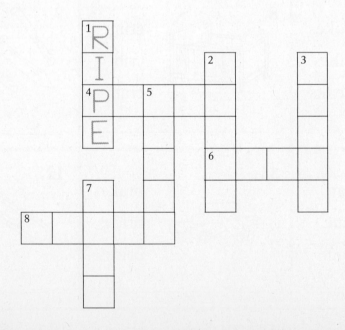

Phonics Home Activity: Ask your child to show you only the boxed words at the top of the page. Then have your child read aloud each clue, while you try to guess which word answers it.

Say each picture name. Write **long o** if the picture name has the long *o* sound. Write **short o** if the picture name has the short *o* sound.

b<u>o</u>x

r<u>o</u>pe

1. *short o*	2.	3.	4.
5.	6.	7.	8.
9.	10.	11.	12.
13.	14.	15.	16.

Name _____

Write a word from the box to complete each sentence.

hop	got	woke	spoke	spot
lot	rod	rock	hope	dock

1. I _____*woke*_____ up my brother early this morning.

2. When he saw the fishing _____ in my hand, he smiled.

3. "I _____ we catch some fish," he said.

4. At the end of the _____ was our big boat.

5. We _____ into it carefully.

6. It was quiet, because no one _____ for a long time.

7. "Watch out for the _____ over there!" I yelled.

8. Then we saw a big fish _____ out of the water.

9. We saw a _____ of fish in that place.

10. "This looks like a good _____ !" I said.

Phonics Home Activity: Ask your child to circle the words in which he or she hears the long *o* sound. Then, on a separate sheet of paper, have your child write and illustrate a sentence containing any two of the words.

Circle the word that names each picture. Then
write **long u** if the word has the long *u* sound.
Write **short u** if the word has the short *u* sound.

 m<u>u</u>g

 c<u>u</u>b<u>e</u>

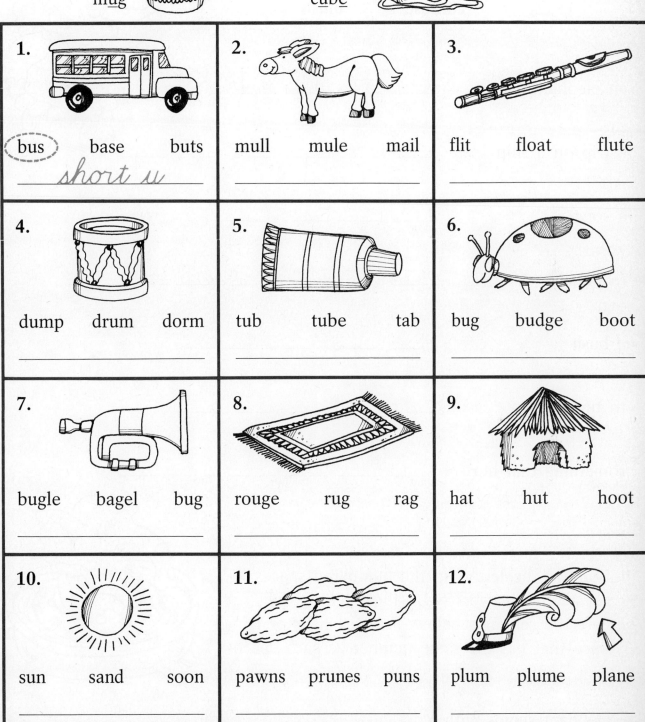

1.

bus   base   buts

short u

2.

mull   mule   mail

_____

3.

flit   float   flute

_____

4.

dump   drum   dorm

_____

5.

tub   tube   tab

_____

6.

bug   budge   boot

_____

7.

bugle   bagel   bug

_____

8.

rouge   rug   rag

_____

9.

hat   hut   hoot

_____

10.

sun   sand   soon

_____

11.

pawns   prunes   puns

_____

12.

plum   plume   plane

_____

Name _____

33

short/long u

Read each meaning. Find the word in the box that goes with each meaning. Then print the word. Put one letter in each space.

shrub	trunk	tune	bruise
cruise	confuse	blush	

1. an elephant's nose   T R U N K
   ₁

2. a trip on a ship   __ __ __ __ __ __
   ₆

3. a song   __ __ __ __
   ₅

4. to puzzle   __ __ __ __ __ __ __
   ₄

5. a bush   __ __ __ __ __
   ₃

6. to turn red   __ __ __ __ __
   ₂

7. something that hurts   __ __ __ __ __ __
   ₇

Now look at the letters in the numbered spaces. If you got all the answers right, those letters will complete the sentence below. Print each letter in the space that has the same number as each space above.

The elephant swims with a __ __ __ __ in a __ __ __ !
1   2   3   4   5   6   7

Phonics Home Activity: Ask your child to make a two-column chart with one column for words with the short *u* sound and one column for words with the long *u* sound. Then have your child copy the nine answer words in the correct columns.

Write the word that completes each sentence.

t<u>ie</u>

ch<u>ie</u>f

flies   **shriek**   **relief**

Pam let out an angry ___*shriek*___

when a bunch of pesty _____

buzzed around her head.

tried   **tied**   **shield**

He _____ to get on his

horse. His _____ was so

heavy he kept falling off.

field   **niece**   **fierce**

Uncle Chan took his _____ Suzi

to the zoo. Suzi was frightened

by the lion's _____ roar.

fried   **pried**   **pier**

We went to the restaurant on the

_____. We ordered

_____ fish and potatoes.

Name _____ **35**

A word that has *ie* in it is hiding in the letters beside each number. A clue to that word is given below the letters. Find the word and circle it. Then print the letters of the word in the boxes.

1. O B N I E C E D L

   the daughter of one's brother or sister

   `N` `I` `E` `C` `E`

2. S F R I E D L Y T R

   a way chicken can be cooked

3. C H I C R I E S L Y

   what a person who is sad does

4. A T S H R I E K C O

   a loud sound

5. S A T R I E D M P

   worked hard at something

6. R E L I E V E P R Y

   to make it hurt less

7. L R M D S H I E L D F

   used to keep the body from getting hurt

What does a man wear with a suit? The letters in the dark boxes spell the answer. Print the answer here.

A ____ ____ ____ ____ ____ ____ ____

Phonics Home Activity: Ask your child to read each word that he or she wrote in the boxes. Then ask your child to try to use each of the words in a sentence.

Circle the word that completes each sentence. Then write the word.

1. A ___moose___ is a big animal.

   moon   (moose)   noon

2. How many people can swim in this _____?

   proof   loop   pool

3. Wear your warm _____ coat.

   woof   wood   wool

4. Is the water deep in this _____?

   brook   broom   brood

5. That glass feels very _____.

   spoon   smooth   smoke

6. I hope this _____ tooth falls out soon.

   loop   spool   loose

7. That sharp _____ can hurt you.

   hook   hoop   hoof

8. I am in the _____ for a good party.

   moon   move   mood

Name _____

Write the word that names the picture. Then write the name in the correct column. Write the name under *book* if the sound for *oo* is the same as it is in *book*. Write it under *boot* if the sound for *oo* is the same as it is in *boot*.

 boot   book

1.  tools tooth tote _tooth_	**2.** hoop hood hook	**3.** spoon spool spook
4. pool pole poor	**5.** wood while wool	**6.** woof wood wide

boot

tooth

_____

_____

book

_____

_____

_____

Phonics Home Activity: Ask your child to read aloud any two words on the page. Then you tell the child if the letters *oo* stand for the same sound in both words. Continue with other words from the page, or with any other words the child chooses.

Write the word that completes each sentence.

cow    bow

crows   gown   crown

The queen had a gold

_____*crown*_____ on her head.

Her _____ was long.

flown   frown   crow

This really works!

A _____ was here a

while ago, but now it has

_____ away.

towel   shown   shower

You are so dirty that you

need a _____.

Here is a clean _____

for you to use.

brow   pillow   frown

You have paint on your face

just above your _____.

Some is on the _____,

too.

Name _____

The answers to the riddles are in the box. Write each answer on the correct line.

your shadow	growing older	paper towels
a crown	snow	your elbow
a flower bed	a crow	a cowboy

1. What rides a horse, but has another animal in his name?

   a cowboy

2. What does a queen wear on her head?

   _____

3. What is part of your arm?

   _____

4. What comes in handy when you spill milk?

   _____

5. What kind of bed should you not sleep in?

   _____

6. What is everyone doing at the same time?

   _____

7. What falls often in winter but never gets hurt?

   _____

8. What follows you on sunny, but not on rainy, days?

   _____

9. What bird is black, but is not a blackbird?

   _____

40 **Phonics Home Activity:** Ask your child to circle the words in which he or she hears the same vowel sound that you hear in *cow*. Then have her or him use each word in an original oral sentence.

Say each picture name. Fill in the circle next to the word that names the picture.

★
- ○ choose
- ○ crowd
- ● chief

1.
- ○ cool
- ○ clown
- ○ cries

2.
- ○ pie
- ○ proof
- ○ power

3.
- ○ booth
- ○ brief
- ○ bowl

4.
- ○ hoot
- ○ hook
- ○ howl

5.
- ○ stow
- ○ steal
- ○ stool

6.
- ○ collie
- ○ cool
- ○ cow

7.
- ○ brown
- ○ brief
- ○ brook

8.
- ○ cries
- ○ cows
- ○ coops

9.
- ○ snow
- ○ spies
- ○ snoop

10.
- ○ spied
- ○ shown
- ○ spoon

11.
- ○ plow
- ○ pool
- ○ plied

12.
- ○ mower
- ○ moose
- ○ movie

13.
- ○ cow
- ○ crow
- ○ cook

14.
- ○ flies
- ○ flows
- ○ fowl

©

Number right _____

Name _____

41

check

Fill in the circle next to the word that completes each sentence.

★ We get _____ from sheep.
○ wilt   ○ wail   ● wool

1. Gary drew a very funny _____.
○ cotton   ○ cartoon   ○ cried

2. Julie's father _____ the fish for supper.
○ fried   ○ frowned   ○ fooled

3. Sally cooked hamburger and _____.
○ needles   ○ narrows   ○ noodles

4. Rob likes to sleep with his head on a _____.
○ pillow   ○ puddle   ○ poodle

5. Tom cut the grass with a _____.
○ moose   ○ movie   ○ mower

6. Have you ever _____ in an airplane?
○ foil   ○ flown   ○ foam

Number right _____ ©

Circle the word that names each picture. Then write the word.

h<u>ay</u>    p<u>ai</u>nt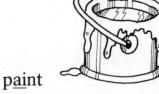

1.	2.	3.
mall may (mail)	trains tries trays	snail style sill
mail		

4.	5.	6.
brides braids brays	chin chant chain	sprite spray sprain

7.	8.	9.
nil knoll nail	runs rays rage	trim trance train

10.	11.	12.
till tail tall	says stale sail	ply play plan

Name _____

ai/ay

Find the word in the box that goes with each meaning. Print the word, putting one letter in each space.

clay	raise	pain	ray	snail
gray	brain	jail	pay	stain

1. a feeling of hurt   P A I N
2. a line of light from the sun   _ _ _
3. a mixture of black and white   _ _ _ _
4. what you use to think   _ _ _ _ _
5. a spot that will not come out   _ _ _ _ _
6. to lift   _ _ _ _ _
7. thing at a police station   _ _ _ _
8. a craft material   _ _ _ _
9. to use money in a store   _ _ _
10. a very slow animal   _ _ _ _ _

Now look at the letters in the black box. If you got all the answers right, those letters will complete the answer to this question:

What do the animals do when they clap their hands?

They ___ ___ ___ ___ ___ the dancing ___ ___ ___ ___ !

Phonics Home Activity: Have your child write the twelve *ai/ay* words on this page as you read each one aloud. Ask your child to tell what letters in each word stand for the long *a* sound. Then have your child name other words in which *ai* or *ay* stand for the long *a* sound.

Circle the word that names the picture. Then write the word.

p<u>oi</u>nt   b<u>oy</u>

1.	foam (foil) fail _foil_	2.	noise nose none	3.	joined joy jar
4.	own out oil	5.	cowboy court coiled	6.	spoil soil sly
7.	bone boil bail	8.	velvet vote voice	9.	ties toil toys
10.	buyer broil brace	11.	royal ruin rooster	12.	coy cooks coins

©

Name _____

oi/oy

Below are some riddles. The answers are in the box. Find the answer to each riddle and write it on the line.

boiling water	coins	your voice
noisy children	a bellboy	a royal family
join parades	a choice	

1. What do people who like to march do?

   join parades

2. What is heard in a crowded playground?

   _____

3. Who carries suitcases but doesn't make a ringing sound?

   _____

4. What can have a king, a queen, a prince, and a princess?

   _____

5. What can be very soft and very loud?

   _____

6. What are hard to save but easy to spend?

   _____

7. What has bubbles and is very hot?

   _____

8. What is sometimes hard to make?

   _____

46

Phonics Home Activity: Ask your child to read each question and the answer he or she wrote. Then have your child circle the letters that stand for the *oi/oy* vowel sound in each answer he or she wrote. You may also ask your child to make up some new riddles to go with the words in the box at the top of the page.

Circle the word that completes each sentence. Then write the word.

1. Would you like ____*toast*____ for breakfast?
   toad   coach   (toast)

2. My _____ hurt, so I called my doctor.
   toaster   throat   toots

3. That _____ is for dinner tonight.
   roost   roast   roads

4. We made two _____ of bread.
   loaves   loans   leaves

5. He never _____ about his big house.
   boils   boats   boasts

6. A _____ looks a little like a frog.
   totes   toad   toast

7. The _____ fell into the sink.
   soap   soak   soup

8. We are moving to the east _____.
   coach   coats   coast

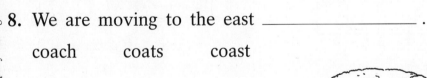

oa

Find the word in the box that goes with each clue.
Write the word.

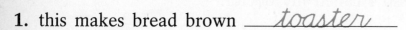

loaves	throat	toaster	croak
roast	soak	coach	toad

1. this makes bread brown _toaster_

2. frogs do this _____

3. person who helps a team _____

4. shapes for bread _____

5. body part _____

6. small animal _____

7. keep very wet _____

8. one way to cook food _____

Now use the words you just wrote in this puzzle.
Print each word next to the number of the clue.

Phonics Home Activity: Ask your child to show you only the boxed words at the top of the page. Then have your child make up clues for each word, while you try to guess which word should answer them.

Read the sentences and look at the pictures. Print
A next to the sentence that tells about Picture **A**.
Print **B** next to the sentence that tells about Picture **B**.

scr<u>ew</u>

A boy <u>drew</u> this barn.   A

I read the <u>news</u> in this.   B

A.   **B.**

This <u>stew</u> is very hot.   ____

A <u>screw</u> fell out of this.   ____

A.   **B.**

Dad <u>blew</u> the light out.   ____

These are wet with <u>dew</u>.   ____

A.   **B.**

I am his <u>nephew</u>.   ____

Did you see the <u>newt</u>?   ____

A.   **B.**

It <u>flew</u> over the school.   ____

Where is the <u>jewel</u>?   ____

A.   **B.**

We <u>threw</u> it away.   ____

The <u>crew</u> is large.   ____

A.   **B.**

©

ew

The answer to each of these riddles is a "Funny Bunny." Each answer is two words that rhyme. Pick one word from **Box A** and one word from **Box B** to complete each riddle. You will use each word only once.

BOX A

shoe	newt	too	new	Two
cruel	Crew's	dew	blue	

BOX B

jewel	screw	few	drew
goo	News	boot	chew	stew

1. What is something you've never eaten before?

   a _*new chew*_

2. What might be the name of a ship's newspaper?

   The _____

3. What is footwear for a small animal?

   a _____

4. What would a mean but valuable stone be?

   a _____

5. What is mud that forms after dew falls?

   _____

6. What fastener might hold a shoe together?

   a _____

7. What sentence tells how many people worked on a picture together?

   _____

8. What phrase means "not enough"?

   _____

9. What is a thick blueberry soup?

   a _____

Phonics Home Activity: Read each of the words containing *ew* aloud to your child and have your child write them. Ask your child to tell what sound these letters stand for in each word. Your child may enjoy thinking up other "funny bunny" riddles using other pairs of rhyming words.

Circle the word that names each picture. Then
write **long e** if the word has the long *e* sound.
Write **short e** if the word has the short *e* sound.

leaf    bread

---

1.    sell   (seal)   sale   *long e*

---

2.    sweeten   swerve   sweater   _____

---

3.    had   head   heed   _____

---

4.   tread   third   thread   _____

---

5.   wrath   wreath   worth   _____

---

6.    feather   father   further   _____

---

7. 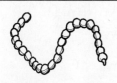   beds   breads   beads   _____

---

8.    mate   meat   met   _____

Name _____

ea

Read this story. Then follow the directions below it.

A careless bat wasn't looking where he was flying, and he crashed into a bush. A coyote leaped out of the bush and grabbed the bat.

"You'll make a fine meal, Mouse," said the coyote. The bat caught his breath to speak.

"Don't eat me, Coyote," pleaded the bat. "I'm not a mouse. Look at my wings! A mouse doesn't have wings. I'm just a little bird."

The surprised coyote let the bat go.

The bat tried to be more careful after that. But one day a fox sneaked up on him and caught him in a meadow. "You'll make a fine feast for me tonight, Little Bird," said the fox.

"I'm not a bird!" squeaked the bat. "Look! All birds have feathers, but I don't. I'm just a mouse. I'm not good for you to eat."

The surprised fox let the bat go again.

"I wish I weren't so careless," thought the bat, "but at least I'm a good talker!"

Underline the word that completes each sentence. Then write the word in the space.

1. A coyote _____leaped_____ out of the bush.

   breath   leaped   squeaked

2. "Don't eat me," the bat _____.

   pleaded   meal   sneaked

3. A fox caught the bat in a _____.

   weak   meadow   breath

4. The bat said he was not a bird because he had no _____.

   meadow   feast   feathers

Phonics Home Activity: Ask your child to find the thirteen different words in this story that contain the letters *ea* together. Have your child make a two-column chart and list the words according to whether *ea* stands for the sound in *bread* (short *e*) or in *meal* (long *e*).

Say each picture name. Fill in the circle next to the word that names the picture.

★
- ○ chair
- ● chain
- ○ cheer

1.
- ○ toad
- ○ tooth
- ○ toaster

2.
- ○ screw
- ○ scram
- ○ scare

3.
- ○ cooks
- ○ coals
- ○ coins

4.
- ○ feature
- ○ feather
- ○ fiesta

5.
- ○ brains
- ○ breaks
- ○ braids

6.
- ○ wreath
- ○ wrath
- ○ wreck

7.
- ○ spread
- ○ speak
- ○ spray

8.
- ○ sofa
- ○ soup
- ○ soap

9.
- ○ soul
- ○ seam
- ○ seal

10.
- ○ couch
- ○ coach
- ○ coat

11.
- ○ thread
- ○ threw
- ○ throat

12.
- ○ royal
- ○ rail
- ○ routine

13.
- ○ tree
- ○ true
- ○ tray

14.
- ○ jewels
- ○ juice
- ○ jealous

©

Number right _____

Name _____

check

Fill in the circle next to the word that completes the sentence.

★ Carol baked four _____ of bread.

   ● loaves   ○ loams   ○ leaves

1. You should always _____ your food well.

   ○ chase   ○ chew   ○ clue

2. Why did Jane tie that rope around her _____?

   ○ white   ○ wealth   ○ waist

3. My grandmother knitted this warm _____ for me.

   ○ swing   ○ sweater   ○ sweet

4. Leon _____ his friends on the stage.

   ○ joined   ○ joyful   ○ juggled

5. We heard a mouse _____ in the attic.

   ○ sulking   ○ steaming   ○ squeaking

6. My new coat is _____, not black.

   ○ grown   ○ grease   ○ gray

7. Jon is a good and _____ friend.

   ○ leash   ○ loyal   ○ loiter

8. We walked home in the rain and got _____.

   ○ soaked   ○ soiled   ○ spoiled

9. Nick is Mrs. Arnez's _____.

   ○ note   ○ nephew   ○ necklace

Number right _____

Phonics Home Activity: Ask your child to read the completed sentences. Then have your child choose two of the sentences to copy and illustrate on a separate piece of paper.

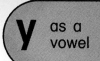

Write the word that completes each sentence.

fl<u>y</u>    cherr<u>y</u>

shiny   tying   skinny

Leo was _____*tying*_____ his sneaker.

He spotted something _____.

It was a silver dollar.

shy   cloudy   sky

Lori looked up at the _____.

"It's very _____," she said.

"I think it may rain."

busy   motorcycle   bumpy

Tim's father has a _____.

He took Tim for a ride in the country.

The country road was _____.

melody   lying   messy

Ana was _____ on her bed.

She was listening to the radio.

Ana heard her favorite _____.

Name _____

Below are some riddles. The answers are in the box. Find the answer to each riddle and write it on the line.

on a windy day	daisy	a teddy bear
a pokey puppy	a sly fox	reply quickly
a lucky penny	a silly rhymer	a funny bunny

1. What do people who get party invitations do?

   reply quickly

2. When is it hard to keep your hat on?

   _____

3. What kind of animal lives in a toy store window?

   _____

4. What kind of animal hops backwards?

   _____

5. What can be the name of a flower or a girl?

   _____

6. Who might say something like "pink ink"?

   _____

7. What kind of coin might you spend on a wish?

   _____

8. What might you call someone who is tricky?

   _____

9. What is another name for a slow, young dog?

   _____

Phonics Home Activity: Ask your child to read each question and the answer he or she wrote. Then have your child circle the letter *y* in each answer and tell whether it stands for the long *i* sound or the long *e* sound. Have your child make up some new riddles to go with the words in the box at the top of the page.

Write the word that completes each sentence.

find night

wind   blind   right

Sue has a music box.

It's in her ___*right*___ hand.

She is about to _____ it.

might   remind   tight

"Hi, Annie. This is Bob. I'm calling

to _____ you about the

game tomorrow. I think we

_____ win this one."

flight   slight   behind

Mr. Carr is at the airport.

He is standing _____ two people.

He thinks he may miss his _____.

sight   frightened   hind

There was a sudden loud noise.

The noise _____ the horse.

It stood on its _____ legs.

Name _____

57

ind, ight

Find the word in the box that goes with each clue. Write the word.

right	mind	night	behind
kind	flight	wind	delighted

1. what we do to some watches _____wind_____

2. very happy _____

3. opposite of day _____

4. what you use to think _____

5. in back of _____

6. an airplane trip _____

7. correct _____

8. thoughtful of others _____

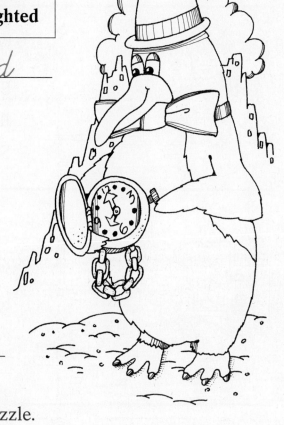

Now use the words you just wrote in this puzzle. Print each word next to the number of the clue.

Phonics Home Activity: Ask your child to read each clue and the answer he or she wrote. Then have your child circle the letters that stand for the sounds for *ind* and *ight*.

Circle the word that names the picture. Then write the word.

ladder   shirt   turtle

car   corn

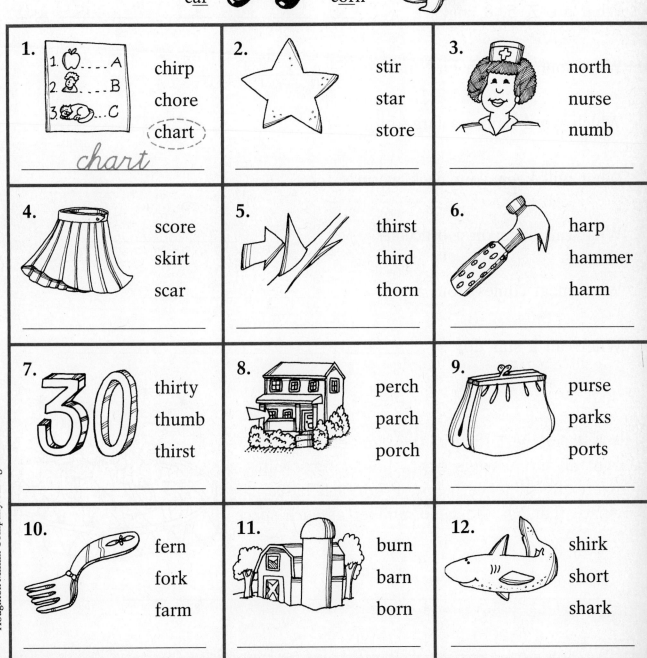

1. chirp
   chore
   (chart)

   chart

2. stir
   star
   store

3. north
   nurse
   numb

4. score
   skirt
   scar

5. thirst
   third
   thorn

6. harp
   hammer
   harm

7. thirty
   thumb
   thirst

8. perch
   parch
   porch

9. purse
   parks
   ports

10. fern
    fork
    farm

11. burn
    barn
    born

12. shirk
    short
    shark

Name _____

vowel plus *r*

Find the word in the box that answers each question. Then print the word. Put one letter in each space.

turkey	numbers	pork	scarf
chirp	charm	sparkle	

1. What are 7, 5, 8, and 6? N U M B E R S
                7   5   17

2. What sound does a bird make? ____ ____ ____ ____ ____
            12 1 13

3. Which word names a large bird? ____ ____ ____ ____ ____ ____
             16 3

4. What will keep your neck warm? ____ ____ ____ ____ ____
        6 15   9

5. What can hang on a bracelet? ____ ____ ____ ____ ____
       10 11   14

6. What meat comes from a pig? ____ ____ ____ ____
        2

7. What can a star do? ____ ____ ____ ____ ____ ____ ____
      4   8

Now look at the letters in the numbered spaces. If you got all the answers right, those letters will complete the sentence below. Print each letter in the space that has the same number as each space above.

The ____ ____ ____ ____ ____ ____ ____ ____ ____ ____ ____
    1 2 3 4 5 6 7 8 9 10 11

at the ____ ____ ____ ____ ____ ____ !
    12 13 14 15 16 17

Phonics Home Activity: Ask your child to make a five column chart, one column for each vowel letter plus *r*. Then have your child copy the ten answer words in the correct columns.

Write a word to complete each sentence.

sincere   cure   severe

He is not too sick, but
he has a ___*severe*___ cold.
A week in bed will _____
him.

entire   beware   chores

Don't wait for me.
I must do my _____.
I have to finish cleaning my
_____ room.

wire   tore   wore

Can you fix these pants?
I _____them to the
park. They _____
on a nail.

pasture   pure   hire

I can't do all the work myself.
I will _____ someone to
help me fix the fence around
the _____.

Name _____

vowel plus *re*

Find the word in the box that goes with each clue. Write the word.

bored	bare	tired	secure
sincere	wire	square	snore

1. empty *bare*

2. noise a sleeper makes _____

3. shape of a box _____

4. safe _____

5. needing sleep _____

6. this is thin and strong _____

7. has nothing to do _____

8. real and true _____

Now find each word you just wrote in this puzzle. Draw a line around each word. The words go → and ↓.

```
W  B  A  R  E  S  B  T
I  S  E  C  D  Q  A  I
R  T  S  E  C  U  R  E
E  T  Q  P  L  A  N  S
S  I  N  C  E  R  E  N
B  R  R  O  A  E  N  O
O  E  B  O  R  E  D  R
R  D  A  K  S  Q  U  E
```

Phonics Home Activity: Ask your child to read aloud each word that she or he found. Then have him or her hunt for other words. (*barn, clear, cook, plans*)

Say each picture name. Fill in the circle next to the
word that names the picture.

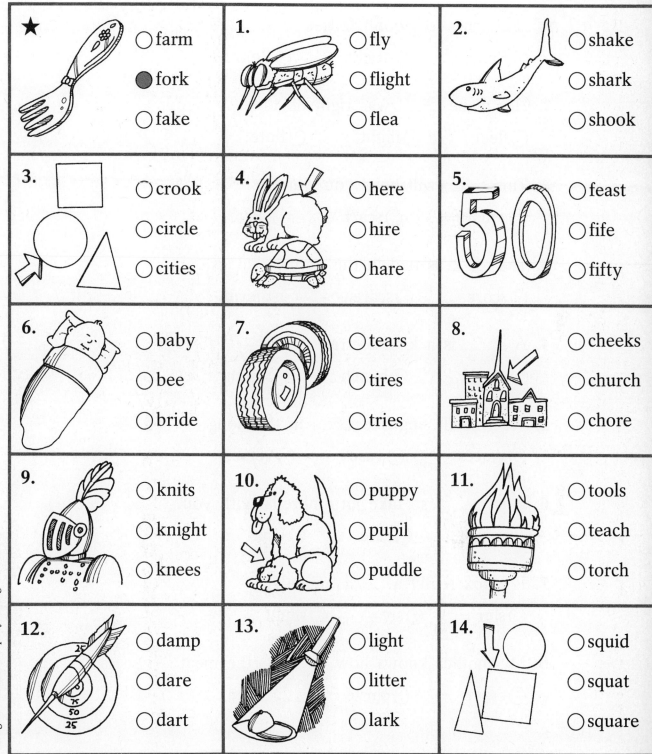

★
○ farm
● fork
○ fake

1.
○ fly
○ flight
○ flea

2.
○ shake
○ shark
○ shook

3.
○ crook
○ circle
○ cities

4.
○ here
○ hire
○ hare

5.
○ feast
○ fife
○ fifty

6.
○ baby
○ bee
○ bride

7.
○ tears
○ tires
○ tries

8.
○ cheeks
○ church
○ chore

9.
○ knits
○ knight
○ knees

10.
○ puppy
○ pupil
○ puddle

11.
○ tools
○ teach
○ torch

12.
○ damp
○ dare
○ dart

13.
○ light
○ litter
○ lark

14.
○ squid
○ squat
○ square

©

Number right _____

Name _____

Fill in the circle next to the word that completes each sentence.

★ _____ me, so I don't forget.
○ Rainy   ○ Right   ● Remind

1. Her plane _____ was right on time.
○ fleet   ○ flight   ○ flute

2. This _____ will keep you warm.
○ square   ○ scarf   ○ skate

3. The _____ is tied in this game.
○ score   ○ scare   ○ squirm

4. A _____ is a kind of tree.
○ bored   ○ bench   ○ birch

5. We will all sing one _____ in this song.
○ voices   ○ vase   ○ verse

6. It is _____, so take an umbrella with you.
○ rainy   ○ rare   ○ rind

7. Is a fox really a _____ animal?
○ slur   ○ sly   ○ slight

8. My mother knows how to _____ the meat.
○ crave   ○ curve   ○ carve

Number right _____

Phonics Home Activity: Ask your child to read the sentences that she or he has completed. Then have your child explain why the other word choices were not correct.

Say the picture name in each box. Write the letters that stand for the beginning sounds.

broom   crown   dragon   tree

frog   grass   princess

1. _cr_ ib	**2.** _____ ess	**3.** _____ ush	**4.** _____ ay
5. _____ ame	**6.** _____ ize	**7.** _____ um	**8.** _____ ayon
9. _____ acks	**10.** _____ etzel	**11.** _____ ick	**12.** _____ apes
13. _____ ink	**14.** _____ ince	**15.** _____ ick	**16.** _____ ead

Name _____

65

Use a word from **Box A** and a word from **Box B** to write two-word phrases to go with each meaning. Each of the two words in every answer will begin with the same cluster with *r*. Use each word only once.

BOX A

cross	drowsy	frozen
drab	brown	crazy
grateful	broiled	
frisky	trout	

BOX B

fruit	dragon	bracelet
crow	frog	trot
broccoli	grin	
drama	crab	

1. something to wear on your arm   a *brown bracelet*

2. an angry sea animal   a _____

3. a sleepy monster   a _____

4. a playful jumper   a _____

5. a thankful smile   a _____

6. a dance for a fish   a _____

7. a silly bird   a _____

8. cooked vegetables   _____

9. a boring play   a _____

10. icy strawberries   _____

Phonics Home Activity: Read aloud to your child each of the words in the boxes at the top of the page. Ask your child to name the two-letter cluster that begins each word. Then ask your child to write each word, circling the cluster at the beginning of each one.

Circle the word that names each picture. Write the word on the line. Then underline the cluster at the beginning of the word you have written.

<u>f</u>lag

<u>pl</u>ate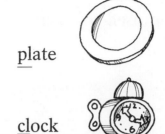

<u>gl</u>ass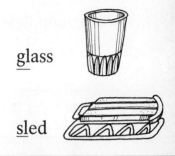

<u>bl</u>ock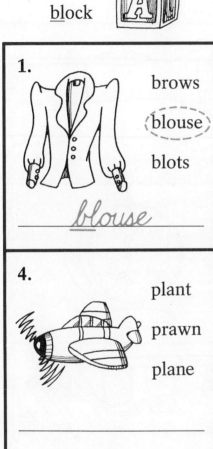

<u>cl</u>ock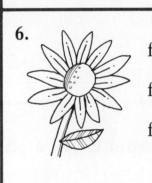

<u>sl</u>ed

1.
brows
(blouse)
blots

blouse

2.
glove
grove
gulf

_____

3.
slats
slacks
stacks

_____

4.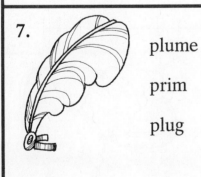
plant
prawn
plane

_____

5.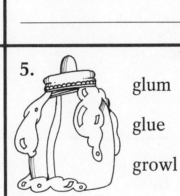
glum
glue
growl

_____

6.
flute
flower
fuller

_____

7.
plume
prim
plug

_____

8.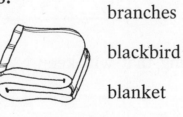
branches
blackbird
blanket

9.
clam
crane
clown

Name _____

67

Each sentence tells about a word that begins with a cluster with *l*. The word is hiding in the letters. Find the word and circle it. Then print the word.

1. This word names something used to hang clothes on a line.

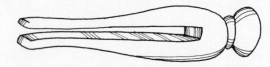

t r c l o t h e s p i n e g   c l o t h e s p i n

2. This word names something that will help you find your way in the dark.

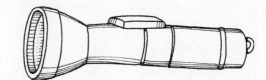

f l a s h l i g h t g l a   _ _ _ _ _ _ _ _ _ _

3. This word names a round map of the world.

p l g l o b e n g   _ _ _ _ _ _

4. This word names a place for fun!

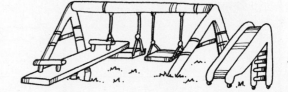

e g p l a y g r o u n d g l   _ _ _ _ _ _ _ _ _ _

5. This word names something that will keep your feet warm.

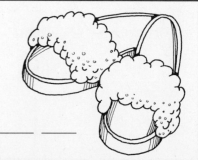

l e s l i p p e r s l e   _ _ _ _ _ _ _ _

Phonics Home Activity: Have your child write the five answer words and circle the cluster that begins each one. Then have your child write these words as you read each one: *sleep, please, sell, glass, pail, grass, fly, clam, came, block, fill, back*. Have your child circle those words that begin with a cluster with *l*.

Say each picture name. Write the letters that stand for the beginning sounds or ending sounds.

scarf   sled   smile   snowflake   spoon

1. sm___ ock	**2.** ____ ide	**3.** ____ ale	**4.** ____ ider
5. ____ eeve	**6.** ____ arecrow	**7.** ____ eakers	**8.** ____ acks

skate   star   vest   swim

9. ____ apler	**10.** ____ eleton	**11.** ____ ans	**12.** fi ____
13. ____ eater	**14.** toa ____	**15.** ____ is	**16.** ____ adium

Name _____

69

clusters with *s*

Read each sentence. Circle the picture that goes with it. Then write the underlined word.

1. The <u>skunk</u> went under the house.

skunk

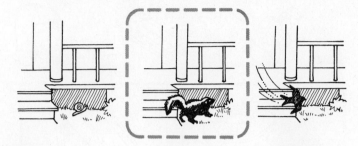

2. Joan <u>sniffed</u> the flowers.

_____

3. Tina has a small <u>scar</u>.

_____

4. Sue put a bow around her <u>wrist</u>.

_____

5. This is very <u>smooth</u>.

_____

6. The horse is in the <u>stable</u>.

_____

Phonics Home Activity: Ask your child to read each sentence on the page, point to the correct picture and explain why the other two pictures are not correct. Then, on a separate sheet of paper, have your child write new sentences for two of the underlined words and then illustrate them.

Circle each picture name. Then print the letters that stand for the beginning sounds.

string   three 3   spray

1.   trade   threw   (thread)   t h r

2.   strap   straw   strut   ___ ___ ___

3.   thorn   throne   stroke   ___ ___ ___

4.   spruce   spring   stretch   ___ ___ ___

5.   sprint   sprinkler   struggle   ___ ___ ___

6.   stroller   stretcher   sprinkler   ___ ___ ___

7.   throat   throw   thrift   ___ ___ ___

Name _____   71

spr/str/thr

Find the word in the box that goes with each meaning. Then print the word. Put one letter in each space.

string	sprint	throat
throne	spruce	strong

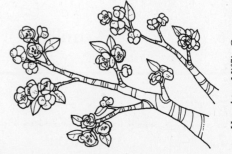

1. to run fast a short way

S P R I N T

2. a kind of tree

_ _ _ _ _ _

3. part of the body

_ _ _ _ _ _

4. something you can tie

_ _ _ _ _ _

5. something to sit on

_ _ _ _ _ _

6. able to lift heavy things

_ _ _ _ _ _

Now look at the letters in the black boxes. If you got all the answers right, those letters will make another word. This word means "the time after winter." What is the word?

_ _ _ _ _ _

Phonics Home Activity: Ask your child to write the words in the box at the top of the page as you read each one aloud. Ask your child to tell what three-letter cluster begins each word. Then help your child to look in a newspaper or magazine to find and cut out other words that begin with *spr, str,* or *thr.*

Say each picture name. Fill in the circle next to the letters that stand for the beginning sounds.

★
- ○ sc
- ● st
- ○ str

1.
- ○ bl
- ○ sh
- ○ br

2.
- ○ sh
- ○ sk
- ○ st

3.
- ○ st
- ○ str
- ○ sp

4.
- ○ st
- ○ str
- ○ sh

5.
- ○ thr
- ○ th
- ○ tr

6.
- ○ co
- ○ cl
- ○ cr

7.
- ○ br
- ○ bo
- ○ bl

8.
- ○ cr
- ○ cl
- ○ sc

9.
- ○ pl
- ○ ph
- ○ pr

10.
- ○ sl
- ○ sn
- ○ sk

11.
- ○ th
- ○ tr
- ○ thr

12.
- ○ st
- ○ str
- ○ sw

13.
- ○ sn
- ○ sl
- ○ spr

14.
- ○ pr
- ○ pl
- ○ ph

©

Number right _____

Name _____

73

check

Fill in the circle next to the word that completes each sentence.

★ Jim _____ the dirt off the floor.
○ spoke   ● swept   ○ stopped

1. We must be _____ or we will miss the train.
○ prompt   ○ promise   ○ proud

2. Your _____ helps you to lift heavy things.
○ strict   ○ strength   ○ struck

3. People who are _____ spend money carefully.
○ sleek   ○ plain   ○ thrifty

4. Dad cooked the fish in a _____.
○ skinny   ○ skillet   ○ skunk

5. He went to the _____ for a football game.
○ spotlight   ○ stadium   ○ stallion

6. My brother rode his bike to the _____.
○ planet   ○ pledge   ○ playground

Number right _____   ©

Phonics Home Activity: Ask your child to write the answer words as you read each one aloud. Then ask your child to circle the two- or three-letter cluster that stands for the beginning sounds in each word.

Circle the word that names the picture. Then write the word.

queen   squirrel

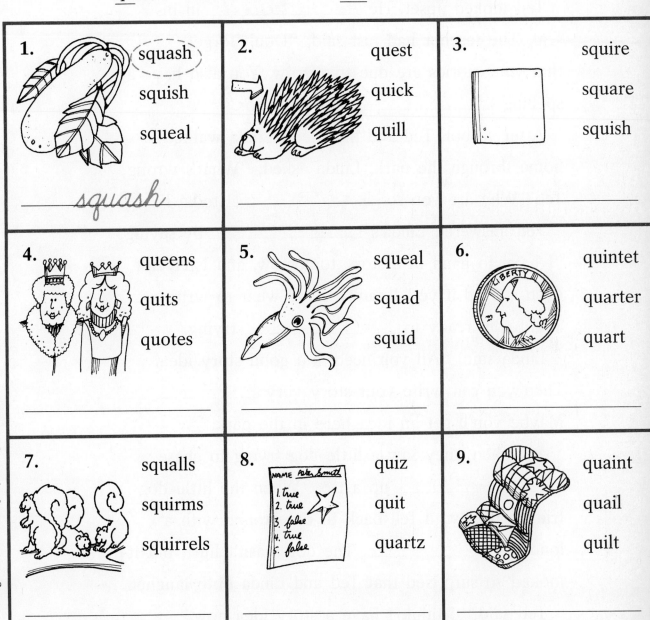

1. (squash) squish squeal

squash

2. quest quick quill

3. squire square squish

4. queens quits quotes

5. squeal squad squid

6. quintet quarter quart

7. squalls squirms squirrels

8. quiz quit quartz

9. quaint quail quilt

Name

qu/squ

Read this story. Write the word from the box that belongs in each space.

questions	squirmed	quiet	quickly
squirrel	quiz	squeal	quit

Ted looked upset. He _squirmed_ in his seat. The teacher had just said, "Don't forget that your stories are due tomorrow. You also have a spelling _____ to study for."

After school, Ted and his friend Linda walked home through the park. Linda asked, "What's wrong, Ted? Why are you so _____ today?"

Ted answered Linda's _____ by saying, "I have to hand in a story tomorrow, and I haven't even started it yet! I can't decide what to write about. I'm ready to _____ trying."

Linda said, "All you need is a good story idea. Then you can write your story very _____. Maybe you'll get an idea here in the park."

Just then, they saw a little dog trying to chase a _____ up a tree. When the little dog tried to follow, it fell back to the ground with a loud _____. The dog wasn't hurt, but it looked so surprised that Ted and Linda both laughed.

Ted said, "I think I have a story idea now."

Phonics Home Activity: Ask your child to read the completed story. Then ask your child to circle the letters that stand for the *qu* or *squ* sound in the words that he or she wrote.

Say each picture name. Then write the letters that stand for the ending sounds.

swing <u>ng</u>   skunk

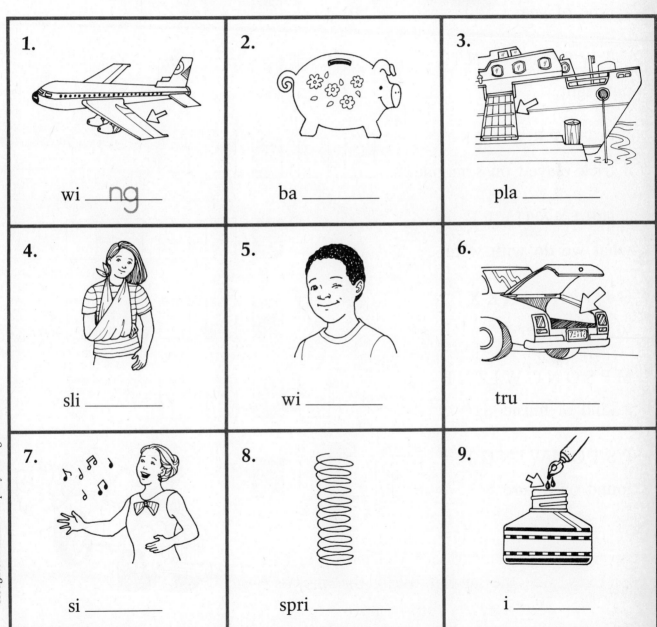

1. wi <u>ng</u>

2. ba _____

3. pla _____

4. sli _____

5. wi _____

6. tru _____

7. si _____

8. spri _____

9. i _____

Name _____

ng/nk

A word that has *ng* or *nk* in it is hiding in the letters beside each number. A clue to that word is given below the letters. Find the word and circle it. Then print the letters of the word in the boxes.

1. O Y N B A N G D E Q
   a loud noise

   B A N G

2. T S P R I N G A L I
   a time of year

3. C T W R O N G A N T
   not right

4. Y O T H P R A N K F
   a trick played on someone

5. T D R I N K U V L R
   what we do with water

6. G J O S H R I N K X
   to get smaller

7. M P S O N G W I Z N F
   a kind of music

8. P S T O K W I N G T
   found on a bird

What animal is a bad driver? The letters in the dark boxes spell the answer. Write the answer here.

_____ _____ _____ _____ _____ _____

Phonics Home Activity: Ask your child to read each word that he or she wrote in the boxes. Then ask your child to try to use each of the words in a sentence.

Say each picture name. Write the letters that stand for the beginning sounds.

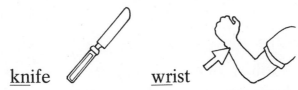

knife   wrist

1. _kn_ ight

2. _____ ench

3. _____ ecker

4. _____ estler

5. _____ uckle

6. _____ eath

7. _____ iter

8. _____ itter

9. _____ ocker

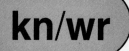

kn/wr

Below are eight riddles. The answers are in the box. Write each answer on the correct line.

wrinkles	knobby ones	wrong	a monkeywrench
the wrapper	knuckles	a knapsack	a knothole

1. What tool belongs in a zoo?

   a monkeywrench

2. What hole is not really a hole?

   _____

3. What do you call the bumps on a hand?

   _____

4. What part of a picnic lunch should you not eat?

   _____

5. What do clothes get that people get, too?

   _____

6. What kind of knees might a door have?

   _____

7. Which sounds as if it might be a sleeping bag?

   _____

8. What word is always spelled wrong?

   _____

Phonics Home Activity: Ask your child to read the riddles aloud to you while you try to guess the answers. Have your child make up other riddles that use the words *knead*, *knot*, and *wrapper* either as part of the question or as part of the answer.

Say each picture name. Write **sh** if the picture name has the sound for *sh*.

shoe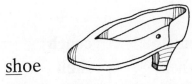

1. _sh_	2.	3.	4.

Write **ch** if the picture name has the sound for *ch*.

cherry

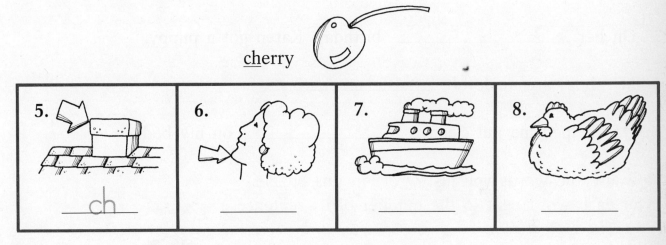

5. _ch_	6.	7.	8.

Write **th** if the picture name has the sound for *th*.

mo<u>th</u>

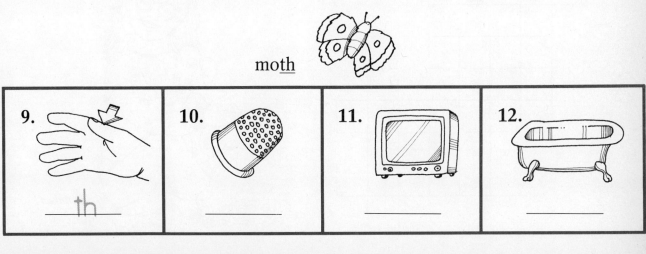

9. _th_	10.	11.	12.

Name _____

81

sh/ch/th

Write a word from the box that completes each sentence.

each	tenth	coach	leather
sheets	ashes	shell	

1. The fire turned the logs into _____*ashes*_____ .

2. Jen found a beautiful _____ at the beach.

3. I have a big breakfast _____ morning.

4. Our _____ will help our baseball team.

5. On her _____ birthday, Karen got a puppy.

6. My shoes are made of _____ .

7. Dad helped me put clean _____ on my bed.

Now use the words you just wrote in this puzzle.
Print each word next to the number of its sentence.

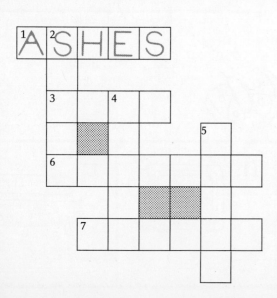

Phonics Home Activity: Have your child read each sentence, telling whether the handwritten word contains *sh*, *ch*, or *th* and what sound those letters stand for. Then have your child make a three-column chart, one column each for *sh*, *ch*, and *th*, and write on the chart other words that have these letters and sounds.

Circle the word that names the picture. Then write the word.

duck    rocket    <u>ph</u>oto    ele<u>ph</u>ant

1.	(nickel) nicked niece *nickel*	2.	sandwich saxophone satisfy	3.	locker local lock
4.	television telegraph telephone	5. 	bundle bunch buckle	6. 	bricks brings breaks
7.	dollar dolphin dough	8. 	pickerel picket pickle	9.	photographer phonograph phone
10. 	trouble trough trophy	11.	click clock cloak	12.	neckerchief nectarine necklace

Name _____

ck/ph

Read this story. Write the word from the box that belongs in each space.

Quickly	photographs	racket	dolphins
pamphlet	chuckle	autograph	photographer
knack	flock	telephone	picked

Jan received a camera for her birthday. The camera came with a _pamphlet_ that told how to take good pictures.

Jan took many _____ . She showed them to her mom. One of them made her mother _____ . It was of three _____ splashing in the waves. "You were lucky to get this picture," her mom said. "What other pictures did you take?"

"Here is one of a _____ of birds," Jan said. "Boy, what a _____ they made when they flew by."

"Jan, you have a real _____ for this," her mom said. "Maybe someday you will be a great _____ . You'll be famous. Everyone will want your _____ . Newspapers from all over will want to hire you. The _____ will never stop ringing."

"Well, in that case," Jan said as she _____ up her camera, "I should take more great pictures."

_____ , she snapped some pictures of her mom.

Phonics Home Activity: Ask your child to read the completed story. Then ask him or her to circle the letters that stand for the *ck* or *ph* sound in the words that he or she wrote.

Say each picture name. Fill in the circle next to the word that names the picture.

★
- ○ cheer
- ● cherry
- ○ check

1.
- ○ shack
- ○ shameful
- ○ shadow

2.
- ○ leash
- ○ learn
- ○ lease

3.
- ○ threw
- ○ thrash
- ○ thread

4.
- ○ megaphone
- ○ microphone
- ○ microscope

5.
- ○ check
- ○ cheek
- ○ chick

6.
- ○ wreath
- ○ wrath
- ○ wreck

7.
- ○ brick
- ○ brash
- ○ brush

8.
- ○ photograph
- ○ phonograph
- ○ phone

9.
- ○ shall
- ○ shelf
- ○ shell

10.
- ○ couch
- ○ coach
- ○ coat

11.
- ○ thumb
- ○ thimble
- ○ thump

12.
- ○ neck
- ○ nice
- ○ nickel

13.
- ○ chime
- ○ chimney
- ○ chummy

14.
- ○ shower
- ○ show
- ○ share

Number right _____

Name _____

Fill in the circle next to the word that completes the sentence.

★ You may use my _____ to wash your hair.
○ shadow   ● shampoo   ○ shameful

1. I read the first two _____ of this book.
○ chapters   ○ channels   ○ chariots

2. This _____ just arrived for you in the mail.
○ pancake   ○ pocket   ○ package

3. The king is sitting on his _____.
○ thimble   ○ through   ○ throne

4. Write two _____ about your vacation.
○ photographs   ○ paragraphs   ○ parasites

5. Jack woke up late so he had to _____.
○ rash   ○ rushed   ○ rush

6. We looked down at the river from the _____.
○ bride   ○ bridge   ○ brain

7. This bracelet is not _____ very much money.
○ worth   ○ wealth   ○ worthy

8. Peter is Mrs. Johnson's _____.
○ necklace   ○ nephew   ○ napkin

9. Everyone laughed when the ducks _____.
○ quaked   ○ quickened   ○ quacked

Number right _____

Phonics Home Activity: Ask your child to read the completed sentences. Then have your child choose two of the sentences to copy and illustrate on a separate piece of paper.

Fill in the missing letters in the alphabet below.

A   B   C   D   ___   F   G   H   ___

J   ___   L   ___   N   O   ___   Q   R

___   T   ___   V   ___   X   ___   ___

Below are some questions about alphabetical order.
Print the letter that answers each question.

1. What letter comes after G? _____

2. What letter comes before U? _____

3. What letter comes after Q? _____

4. What letter comes before O? _____

5. What letter comes after H? _____

6. What letter comes before W? _____

7. What is the last letter in the alphabet? _____

Now cover the top of your paper, and print the
whole alphabet here.

___ ___ ___ ___ ___ ___ ___ ___ ___

___ ___ ___ ___ ___ ___ ___ ___ ___

___ ___ ___ ___ ___

Name _____   **87**

Below are some scrambled sentences. When you put these words in alphabetical order, you will have a sentence that makes sense. Write the sentence on the line. Be sure to use correct punctuation, and to begin your sentence with a capital letter.

1. talk   did   you   with   she

   Did she talk with you?

2. wall   the   I   over   looked

3. that   know   does   word   he

4. me   give   that   don't   worm

5. songs   four   played   together   girls

6. in   careful   water   the   be

7. notebook   my   right   I   left   there

8. many   do   bear   a   tricks   can

Phonics Home Activity: Ask your child to read the completed sentences. Then have your child choose two of the sentences to copy and illustrate on a separate piece of paper.

Read each group of three words. Decide which word in each group comes **first** in the alphabet. Write that word on the line.

1.	2.	3.	4.
thin	ice	sell	break
tell	itch	sale	blow
table	ink	sill	big
table	_____	_____	_____

5.	6.	7.	8.
cry	prompt	scale	dill
clock	play	shell	dell
cove	phrase	space	doll
_____	_____	_____	_____

9.	10.	11.	12.
them	apple	flap	graze
treasure	angel	fresh	ghost
token	artist	fury	gilt
_____	_____	_____	_____

Name _____

89

alphabetical order: second letter

In each group of words, find the word that comes **first** in alphabetical order. Print that word, putting one letter in each space.

1. rubber   rocket   report   r e p o r t
                                            ‾18 ‾9 ‾ ‾ ‾4 ‾

2. piece   party   porch   ‾ ‾ ‾ ‾ ‾
                                           13 2   12

3. dirty   drink   dough   ‾ ‾ ‾ ‾ ‾
                                           15 6

4. usual   under   urban   ‾ ‾ ‾ ‾ ‾
                                           14   16

5. pillow   pretty   please   ‾ ‾ ‾ ‾ ‾ ‾
                                            1   10 17

6. graze   guess   glass   ‾ ‾ ‾ ‾ ‾
                                           7   11   8

7. sink   slip   ship   ‾ ‾ ‾ ‾
                                              3 5

If you got all the answers right, the numbered letters will complete the sentence below. Print each letter in the space that has the same number as each space above. The words that you make will be in alphabetical order.

A ‾ ‾ ‾ ‾ of ‾ ‾ ‾ ‾
  1 2 3 4   5 6 7 8

‾ ‾ ‾ ‾ in a ‾ ‾ ‾ ‾ ‾ ‾ !
9 10 11 12   13 14 15 16 17 18

Each group of words should be in alphabetical order. Circle the word that belongs in each space. Then write the word in the space.

1. bake, _____*ball*_____, bark, bat

   bad   baby   (ball)

2. facts, _____, farm, fasten

   faint   face   father

3. chart, cheer, _____, choose

   change   chose   chick

4. difficult, dinner, _____, dishes

   die   dig   dirty

5. crash, cross, crutch, _____

   craft   cry   crayon

Write each group of words in alphabetical order.

6. hitter   hide   hill

   _____*hide, hill, hitter*_____

7. parts   pants   packs

   _____

8. repair   rest   reads

   _____

9. moan   more   money

   _____

Name _____

alphabetical order: third letter

Write each group of names in alphabetical order.

_____

1. Bill   _____*Benny*_____   **2.** Seth   _____

Beth   _____   Sam   _____

Bob   _____   Sally   _____

Benny   _____   Sara   _____

Bonnie   _____   Selena   _____

_____

3. Tina   _____   **4.** Hilary   _____

Terry   _____   Hannah   _____

Tommy   _____   Harry   _____

Tim   _____   Herb   _____

Tess   _____   Henry   _____

_____

5. Write the names of five of your own friends here.

6. Now write those names in alphabetical order.

_____   _____

_____   _____

_____   _____

_____   _____

_____   _____

92 **Phonics Home Activity:** Have your child name as many things as possible that are usually arranged in alphabetical order. Answers may include class lists, names in phone books, records, dictionary entries, cards in a card catalog, and words in an index.

Say each picture name to yourself.
Then circle the number of syllables you hear.

1.

1   2   ③

2.

1   2   3

3.

1   2   3

4.

1   2   3

5.

1   2   3

6.

1   2   3

7.

1   2   3

8.

1   2   3

9.

1   2   3

10.

1   2   3

11.

1   2   3

12.

1   2   3

Name _____

syllables

Read each sentence and say the underlined word. Then write the number of syllables you hear in that word.

1. Did you ask a <u>question</u>? _2_

2. This <u>beach</u> has nice sand. _____

3. Please close that big <u>window</u>. _____

4. I ate a <u>hamburger</u> for lunch. _____

5. What color <u>paint</u> did you use? _____

6. It is the third letter of the <u>alphabet</u>. _____

7. I will eat just one <u>sandwich</u>. _____

8. I will be ten on my next <u>birthday</u>. _____

9. A fish can <u>breathe</u> under the water. _____

10. How deep is the water in this <u>stream</u>? _____

Now add up all the numbers you wrote. _____
Your answer should fit into this riddle.

What has _____ legs and catches flies?
Answer: A baseball team!

Phonics Home Activity: Ask your child to make up questions that have as their answers the underlined words. For example, *What breathes underwater?* Answer: *a fish.* Children may use the information in the sentences or information from their own experience as part of the question.

Use what you know about dividing words into syllables to decide which word names the picture. Circle the word. Then write the word, dividing it into syllables.

1. choke
(cactus)
collar

cac/tus

2. shampoo
shower
shutter

_____

3. barrel
bottom
bullet

_____

4. pillow
pocket
parrot

_____

5. magnet
mirror
metal

_____

6. passes
piglet
puddle

_____

7. ragged
ribbon
runner

_____

8. windows
willow
wallet

_____

9. whisker
wander
walnut

_____

10. perfect
puppet
pattern

_____

11. turkey
tunnel
tennis

_____

12. hisses
helmet
hollow

_____

Name _____

Use what you know about dividing words in syllables to read the words in the box. Use them to complete the sentences.

cartoons	bandage	perfume	circus	donkey
market	muffin	whiskers	tunnel	nervous

1. It's very dark in this ___*tunnel*___!

2. Watch how the cat cleans its _____.

3. The clowns were the best thing we saw at the _____.

4. You should put a _____ on that cut so it will stay clean.

5. Would you like a hot _____ with your breakfast?

6. Look at all the funny _____ in this book.

7. There is a small _____ where you can buy milk and bread.

8. What long ears that _____ has!

9. I'm giving my sister some pretty _____ for her birthday.

10. He was so _____ that he did not fall asleep quickly.

Phonics Home Activity: Ask your child to read you only the boxed words at the top of the page. Then have him or her make up clues for each word, while you try to guess which word is meant.

Use what you know about dividing words into syllables to decide which word completes each sentence. Circle the word and then write it, dividing it into syllables.

1. I am learning how to play the _____*trum/pet*_____ .

   tractor   (trumpet)   tremble

2. Start the race when you hear the _____ .

   startle   scramble   signal

3. That _____ is full of water.

   battle   butcher   barrel

4. We live in the white _____ .

   cottage   cattle   curtain

5. That little animal is a _____ .

   chimney   chatter   chipmunk

6. The paper will cost a _____ .

   quarter   quitter   quilter

7. The horses started to _____ home.

   grumble   giggle   gallop

8. I am saving _____ in a big jar.

   paddles   pennies   puppies

Name _____

Read each sentence. Look at the underlined word. Decide how to divide the underlined word into syllables. Circle each right answer.

1. The cars moved slowly because of the <u>traffic</u>.

   (traf/fic)   traff/ic   tra/ffic

2. The <u>trumpets</u> made a lot of noise.

   tru/mpets   trump/ets   trum/pets

3. Open the <u>curtains</u> and look out the window.

   cur/tains   curt/ains   curtai/ns

4. The <u>winner</u> of the race looked very happy.

   wi/nner   winn/er   win/ner

5. You can use the <u>pillow</u> that is on my bed.

   pill/ow   pi/llow   pil/low

6. When can the <u>barber</u> cut my hair?

   barb/er   bar/ber   ba/rber

7. There is no more <u>shampoo</u> in the bathroom.

   sha/mpoo   shamp/oo   sham/poo

8. Put the <u>tractor</u> in the barn when you are done.

   trac/tor   tra/ctor   tract/or

Phonics Home Activity: Have your child read aloud the sentences to you. After each sentence, choose several words from the sentence and have the child tell the number of syllables in each word.

Read each sentence. Listen for the vowel sound in the first syllable of each underlined word. Circle **long** if you hear a long vowel sound in the first syllable of the underlined word. Circle **short** if you hear a short vowel sound. Then write the underlined word and divide it into syllables.

 ti/ger    tax/i

1. We saw a <u>zebra</u> at the zoo.

(long)   short   *ze/bra*

2. A <u>lemon</u> is a yellow fruit.

long   short   _____

3. A <u>tepee</u> is a type of tent.

long   short   _____

4. We stayed at a <u>motel</u> on our trip.

long   short   _____

5. Gina <u>studies</u> hard.

long   short   _____

6. Jim did a <u>favor</u> for Grandma.

long   short   _____

Read each question. Decide which word in the box answers each one. Write that word and divide it into syllables.

pedal	labor	robin	silent	music

1. What word means hard work? ___*la/bor*___

2. What word names part of a bicycle? _____

3. What word means the opposite of **loud**? _____

4. What word names a bird? _____

5. What word names pretty sounds? _____

Now circle the vowel that appears in the first syllable of each word. Write those letters on the lines below, in the order of the answers. If you got all the answers right, you will solve this riddle!

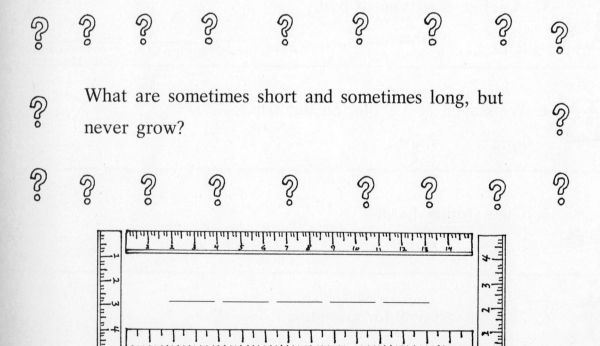

What are sometimes short and sometimes long, but never grow?

___ ___ ___ ___ ___

Phonics Home Activity: Read aloud to your child the following list of words: *balance, cabin, tuba, police, damage, palace, magic,* and *moment.* Have your child tell how many syllables each contains and whether the first syllable contains a long or short vowel sound. Then have your child write each word, showing the syllable break.

Read the sentences and look at the pictures.
Write **A** by the sentence that tells about Picture A.
Write **B** by the sentence that tells about Picture B.
Then write each underlined word and divide it into
syllables.

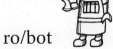 ro/bot   rob/in

 A.   B.

A **1.** I grew a <u>radish</u> in my garden.   _rad/ish_

B **2.** I like to listen to the <u>radio</u>.   _ra/di/o_

 A.   B.

_____ **3.** It is three <u>minutes</u> after four.   _____

_____ **4.** Four <u>minus</u> one is three.   _____

 A.   B.

_____ **5.** This car has a powerful <u>motor</u>.   _____

_____ **6.** This car is only a <u>model</u>.   _____

 A.   B.

_____ **7.** Rosa is working with <u>figures</u>.   _____

_____ **8.** Rosa reads the <u>final</u> page.   _____

Name _____

Read each sentence. Look at the underlined word. Decide how to divide the underlined word into syllables. Circle each right answer.

1. Every person is a different <u>human</u> being with different ideas.

   (hu/man)   hum/an   huma/n

2. This flower has beautiful red <u>petals</u>.

   pe/tals   peta/ls   pet/als

3. Something that is <u>comic</u> is very funny.

   co/mic   com/ic   comi/c

4. My uncle is a <u>grocer</u> who owns a large food store.

   gro/cer   groc/er   gr/ocer

5. Did you buy your dress at a <u>local</u> store or at one far from here?

   loca/l   lo/cal   loc/al

6. I knew you felt cold because I saw you <u>shiver</u>.

   shi/ver   shiv/er   sh/iver

7. I like a slice of <u>lemon</u> in my water.

   lem/on   le/mon   lemo/n

8. Yellow <u>tulips</u> are Sally's favorite flower.

   tul/ips   tu/lips   tuli/ps

Phonics Home Activity: Read aloud to your child each of the underlined words, in random order. Have your child tell how many syllables each contains and whether the first syllable contains a long or short vowel sound. Then have your child write each word, showing the position of the syllable break.

Each of these picture names is a compound word. The first word in the compound is below the picture. Choose the other word and write it on the line to complete the compound word.

basket<u>ball</u>   wrist<u>watch</u>

1. paste brush pick tooth *paste*	**2.** power hair shoe horse _____	**3.** post room spread bed _____
4. port plane tight air _____	**5.** chair band hole arm _____	**6.** shore weed shell sea _____
7. burn fish flower sun _____	**8.** fall melon proof water _____	**9.** ship man pole flag _____
10. room park player ball _____	**11.** gown club fall night _____	**12.** out bird snake black _____

Name _____

You can make a compound word to answer each of the following questions. Pick one word from **BOX A** and one word from **BOX B.** You will use each word only once. Write your compound word on the line following the question.

BOX A

eye	horse	team
hill	snow	space
pine	post	bath
	scare	

BOX B

tub	card	storm
side	brows	ship
back	crow	apple
	mate	

1. What can you write on and send in the mail? *postcard*

2. What person plays on your team? _____

3. What lines of hair are above your eyes? _____

4. What kind of ride can you have on an animal? _____

5. What scares birds in a field? _____

6. What grassy place might be good for a picnic? _____

7. Where is a good place to get clean? _____

8. What can people fly in space? _____

9. What might happen on a cold winter day? _____

10. What is a fruit that you might like to eat? _____

Phonics Home Activity: Read each of the answer choices aloud to your child, emphasizing the two words in each compound. Ask your child to write each word, drawing a line to separate the compound word into its parts.

Write the word that completes each sentence.

stop—sto**pp**ed, sto**pp**ing   smile—smil**ed**   try—t**ries**, t**ried**

call—call**s**   teach—teach**es**

dropping   scared   dropped

The loud noise ___*scared*___

the blackbirds. They _____

the corn and flew away.

flashes   flashing   roars

Thunder _____ like a

hungry lion while lightning

_____ across the sky.

put   arriving   putting

Dora was _____ supper on

the stove to cook just as her mother

was _____ home from work.

copying   copied   hurried

Tim _____ his paper

over. Then he _____

outside to play.

Name _____

107

Read each sentence. Circle the picture that goes with it. Then write the underlined word.

1. The dog is <u>swimming</u> in the pond.

swimming

2. Ana is <u>paying</u> for her ticket.

_____

3. Calvin <u>searches</u> for his shoe.

_____

4. Joan <u>tripped</u> and fell.

_____

5. The children are <u>waving</u>.

_____

6. The King <u>counts</u> his money.

_____

Phonics Home Activity: Ask your child to read each sentence on the page, point to the correct picture and explain why the other two pictures are not correct. Then, on a separate sheet of paper, have your child write new sentences for two of the underlined words and then illustrate them.

Read the sentence and look at the pictures. Print **A** next to the sentence that tells about Picture **A**. Print **B** next to the sentence that tells about Picture **B**.

1. Jay <u>shut</u> the door. _A_

   Jay is <u>shutting</u> the door. _____

   A.    **B.**

2. Grandpa <u>carved</u> a little pig. _____

   Grandpa is <u>carving</u> a little pig. _____

   A.    **B.**

3. The dog is <u>burying</u> the shoe. _____

   The dog <u>buried</u> the shoe. _____

   A.    **B.**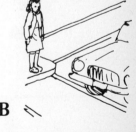

4. Anita will <u>cross</u> the street. _____

   Anita <u>crosses</u> the street. _____

   A.    **B**

5. Mrs. Chung <u>orders</u> lunch. _____

   Mrs. Chung <u>ordered</u> lunch. _____

   A.    **B.**

Name _____

Read the sentences. Then write the word that completes the second sentence.

1. Pedro has a glass of milk.

He is ___*sipping*___ it slowly.

    sipped   sipping

2. Lisa wants the book on the top shelf.

She _____ her arm to reach it.

    stretching   stretches

3. Sara and Carla had a party.

They _____ all of their friends.

    inviting   invited

4. Dan washed the dishes.

Then he _____ them and put them away.

    dries   dried

Phonics Home Activity: Ask your child to read each pair of sentences and explain his or her word choices. Then have your child suggest sentences for the words that were not chosen.

Use what you know about prefixes to read the words in the box. Find the word in the box that matches each meaning. Write the word and circle the prefix.

displeased	unsafe	incorrect	unprepared
inexpensive	replant	dismount	uncertain
incomplete	rejoin		

1. not right ___incorrect___

2. not ready for _____

3. put back in the ground _____

4. get off something _____

5. not sure _____

6. not safe _____

7. go back to the others _____

8. not happy with _____

9. does not cost much money _____

10. not finished _____

Read this story. Use what you know about prefixes to decide which word in the box belongs in each space. Then write the word in the space.

untouched	incomplete	discovered	displeased
recall	unkind	unhappy	inside

My grandfather owns a book store. One day I asked if he had books about pirates. I wanted to learn about treasure maps. Grandpa liked to find books for me. He was never _displeased_ if I asked for one.

"Let me think," said Grandpa. "I _____ that I have one, but it's way in the back."

We found it on a top shelf. It was very dirty. "It looks as if it has been _____ for years," said Grandpa. Then I looked _____ . There, in the back, was an old map.

"It's a real treasure map!" I said. But there was a piece missing. "Oh! It's _____ ! I will not be able to find the treasure," I said. I must have looked pretty _____ , because Grandpa tried to cheer me up.

He said, "I don't mean to be _____ , but think what you did find. You were hoping to find out about treasure maps, but you _____ an old map that might be a pirate's map. Isn't that a treasure?"

I laughed, because he was right.

Use what you know about prefixes to read the answer choices. Then write the word that completes each sentence. Circle the prefix.

1. The paper is *unimportant*, but I want it.
   disrepair   intake   unimportant

2. I have to stay in bed and be _____.
   unsolved   inactive   disbelieving

3. Every six years we _____ the house.
   undo   repaint   dislike

4. What an _____ bird that is!
   uncommon   disinvite   inattention

5. I forgot the names, but I'll _____ them.
   untold   inexact   relearn

6. This shirt is _____, so wear it.
   disrepair   inattention   unwrinkled

7. I like one, but I _____ the other.
   unhitch   dislike   intake

8. Do not let the ball of string _____.
   incomplete   discover   unwind

Name _____

Read each sentence and find the word in it that has a prefix. On the line below, write the word and its meaning.

un-: not, opposite of	**re-: back, again**
in-: not, in or into	**dis-: not, opposite of**

1. My baby sister dislikes people wearing hats.

   dislikes - does not like

2. Do not uncover the paint or it will dry.

   _____

3. When will you repay the money?

   _____

4. This phone is only for incoming calls.

   _____

5. She had a bad fall, but she was unhurt.

   _____

6. I would like to revisit this museum some day.

   _____

7. I think this list is incomplete.

   _____

8. You may see the picture, but it is still unfinished.

   _____

THINGS TO DO
TODAY

1. Feed dog
2. Find book
   for Sally
3. Study for
   spelling test
4. Call...
5.
6.

Write the word that completes each sentence. Then underline the prefix.

<u>a</u>like    <u>be</u>friend    <u>ex</u>claim

1.

aboard   befit   exchange

The two ships were next to one another.

"Come _____*aboard*_____," said the captain.

"We will _____ greetings."

2.

awake   below   explain

Jim cannot sleep.

There is noise _____ his window.

The noise is keeping Jim _____ .

3.

aloud   become   explode

She fills the balloon with air.

The balloon has _____ big.

Do you think it will _____ ?

4.

apart   because   alone

I will help you put it together.

The pieces are _____ now.

I will help _____ I like you!

Name _____

Add the prefix **a-**, **be-**, or **ex-** to each word or word part to make a new word. Write that word. Then draw a line to connect the word with its meaning.

1. a + bed = _____*abed*_____   to shout

2. ex + claim = _____   under

3. a + fire = _____   on fire

4. be + low = _____   to blow up or pop

5. ex + plode = _____   in bed

___

6. a + cross = _____   not with others

7. be + ware = _____   on the other side

8. a + sleep = _____   give to each other

9. ex + change = _____   Watch out!

10. a + lone = _____   not awake

Now find each of the new words in this puzzle. Circle the words. The words go → and ↓ .

```
s  a  f  i  r  e  a  s  t  r
b  a  m  e  x  c  l  a  i  m
e  b  l  t  e  w  o  b  b  n
w  e  x  c  h  a  n  g  e  t
a  d  a  s  l  e  e  p  l  b
r  i  a  c  r  o  s  s  o  e
e  x  p  l  o  d  e  t  w  l
```

Circle the word that will make each sentence tell about the picture. Then write the word on the line and circle the prefix in it.

ahead    below    explode

1. The tree is _____(a)fire_____.

   afire   befriend   explain

2. They _____ to have a good time!

   alike   beware   expect

3. He is happy to _____ this cat!

   abed   befriend   exclaim

4. _____ of the deep hole!

   Apart   Beware   Explain

5. They _____ early in the morning.

   arise   befall   exchange

Name _____ 117

Read this story. Write a word from the box in each space.

exchange	awake	below
explain	across	belong
expect	aloud	because

Jim was staying at his friend Roger's house. He was in the top bed. Roger was sleeping ___*below*___ Jim. But Jim could not sleep at all. He was wide _____. He saw something scary above his head.

Jim told himself not to be scared. But the more he whispered to himself, the worse he felt. Finally he said _____ to Roger, "Will you please _____ places with me? May I come down?"

Roger wanted to go back to sleep. He said, "No, Jim. You _____ up there, and I want to stay here."

"But let me _____ to you what's wrong!" Jim said. "Scary shapes are up here! You can't _____ me to stay up here all alone!"

Roger got out of bed to see the scary shapes. He saw that a bright streetlight _____ the street made a tree seem scary to his friend. He knew it wasn't really scary. But _____ he was a good friend, he traded places with Jim.

Phonics Home Activity: Ask your child to circle the prefix that appears at the beginning of each answer word. Then have your child write a sentence using each word.

Write the word that completes each sentence.

beautif<u>ul</u>   slow<u>ly</u>   stick<u>y</u>

lovely	calmly	buttery	messy	careful
hopeful	badly	thankful	kindly	chewy

1. Maria was _*thankful*_ that no one was hurt.

2. Tom walked _____ onto the stage to give his speech.

3. I love the _____ taste of popcorn.

4. Since it was Lola's first try, she did not do _____.

5. Craig's desk was so _____ he could not find his paper.

6. Sally knew she would have to be _____ as she built her model.

7. Fido loves his _____ dog treats.

8. The flowers my grandfather grows are _____.

9. Celia has _____ offered to take care of my cat.

10. Ted was _____ that he had passed his test.

Name _____

Read each sentence. A word that could replace the underlined words is hiding in the letters. Find the word and circle it. Then write the word on the line and circle the suffix.

1. This bed <u>has lots of lumps</u>. a m l u m p y t e

   _____*lumpy*_____

2. The school bell rings <u>each hour</u>. d e e h o u r l y r t y

   _____

3. The kitten's hair feels <u>like silk</u>. s i t s i l k y m e t

   _____

4. This chicken soup is <u>full of flavor</u>. r u s f l a v o r f u l n t y

   _____

5. Pat was <u>full of care</u> as she treated the sick horse. t e r c a r e f u l r e n

   _____

6. The sky was <u>full of clouds</u>. s u d c l o u d y r e n

   _____

7. Al is <u>having hope</u> about winning the race. h o p e f u l q u e r

   _____

8. Tina visits the city library <u>each week</u>. e r e w e e k l y p r e n

   _____

120 **Phonics Home Activity:** Ask your child to read each sentence and the word he or she wrote on the line. Then have your child choose two of the sentences to copy and illustrate on a separate piece of paper.

Circle the word that will make each sentence tell about the picture. Then write the word on the line. Circle the suffix in each word.

beautif<u>ul</u>   slow<u>ly</u>   stick<u>y</u>

1. Janet's hair is brown and very ___*curly*___ .

   chilly   (curly)   cloudy

2. Chico is a _____ bird.

   nosey   neatly   noisy

3. Tom and Sue are _____ around the house.

   helpful   hopeful   happily

4. The road to the farm was _____ .

   busily   buttery   bumpy

5. Our dog is _____ to everyone.

   foggy   feathery   friendly

6. Chan's new kitten is cute and _____ .

   pitiful   playful   plentiful

Name _____ **121**

Read this story. Write the word from the box that belongs in each space.

closely	barely	daily	loudly	delightful
snowy	wishful	surely	warmly	peaceful

Kenny had a _____wishful_____ look on his face as he listened to the _____ weather report.

"Tomorrow will be cold and _____ ," the announcer said.

"Do you think it could snow so much that we won't have school?" Kenny asked.

The next morning, Kenny jumped out of bed and raced over to the window. "Wow!" he shouted _____ . There was so much snow he could _____ see the back-yard fence. Everything was so quiet and _____ .

"Oh, _____ there will be no school today," Kenny said. Then he went down to the kitchen. His mother had been listening _____ to the "no school" announcements on the radio.

"Well, it seems that you and your sister have the day off," Kenny's mother said.

Later, Kenny and Karen dressed _____ in their winter clothes and went out to play. They spent a _____ day playing in the snow.

Phonics Home Activity: Ask your child to read the completed story. Then ask your child to circle the suffixes in the words that he or she wrote.

Read the words in the box. Think about the base word and the suffix that make up each word. Write the word next to its base word. Circle the suffix.

reality	preparation	direction	loveliest
action	saddest	tasty	certainty
starvation	dirtiest	hungriest	location
hottest	invention	safety	

1. direct _direction_

2. taste _____

3. starve _____

4. real _____

5. sad _____

6. prepare _____

7. certain _____

8. lovely _____

9. dirty _____

10. act _____

11. hot _____

12. locate _____

13. invent _____

14. safe _____

15. hungry _____

Name _____

Use what you know about suffixes to read and understand the words in the box. Then find the word in the box that goes with each clue. Write the word.

1. speed ___*rapidity*___

2. in the least danger _____

3. most dirty _____

4. just an idea _____

5. a number of things _____

6. what really is _____

7. the act of being finished _____

8. the most little _____

| suggestion |
| reality |
| completion |
| dirtiest |
| safest |
| tiniest |
| collection |
| rapidity |

Now use the words you just wrote in this puzzle. Write each word next to the number of the clue.

Use what you know about suffixes to read each answer choice and to write the word that completes each sentence. Circle the suffix.

1. Dad is the _____*tallest*_____ person in our family.
   tasty   transportation   tallest

2. I am helping my sister learn _____.
   subtraction   suggestion   scariest

3. Please pay _____ to what I say.
   angriest   action   attention

4. That certainly was a _____ lunch!
   tasty   tiniest   tightest

5. This is the _____ box I can carry.
   hungriest   heaviest   happiest

6. The _____ is that you are falling.
   perfection   smartest   sensation

7. We counted more than _____ birds.
   ninety   activity   oddity

8. The _____ person ate two sandwiches.
   happiest   hardest   hungriest

Name _____

125

Use what you know about suffixes to read the underlined words in the riddles and their answers. The answers are in the box. Write each answer on the correct line.

in your <u>imagination</u>	a good <u>suggestion</u>
carrying a <u>ninety</u>-one-pound bag	a spelling bee
the tip of an airplane's tail	<u>perfection</u>
the <u>tiniest</u> elephant you ever saw	a cat <u>collection</u>

1. What should you always be ready to take?

a good suggestion

2. What is worse than carrying a <u>ninety</u>-pound bag?

_____

3. Where should you look for good ideas?

_____

4. What is small and gray and lives in a mouse hole?

_____

5. What do you call the number 100 on a test?

_____

6. What is the <u>highest</u> point you can think of?

_____

7. What is the <u>smartest</u> insect of all?

_____

8. What do you call ten cats on a shelf?

_____

Phonics Home Activity: Have your child read the riddles aloud to you while you try to guess the answers. Then work together and try to make up other riddles using the underlined words from the page.

Write the word that completes each sentence. Then underline the suffix.

hair<u>less</u> sick<u>ness</u>  measure<u>ment</u>

1.

sleepless   improvement   darkness

Donna's little dog was crying.

The dog felt alone in the ___*darkness*___ .

Will Donna have a _____ night?

2.

happiness   shipment   hopeless

Do you want to buy a plant?

I just got a big _____ of them.

A plant can bring you much _____ .

3.

sunless   announcement   excitement

We can't wait for the show to start!

Our _____ is growing!

The man is making an _____ .

4.

refreshments   endless   heaviness

We are tired from our hike.

The hike seemed difficult and _____ .

Let's stop for some _____ .

Name _____

Find the word in the box that goes with each meaning. Then print the word. Put one letter in each space.

lightness	statement	hairless	careless	heaviness
endless	development	changeless	dimness	fatness

1. without change   c h a n g e l e s s

2. the act of developing   — — — — — — — — — — —

3. state of being heavy   — — — — — — — — —

4. without care   — — — — — — — —

5. with no hair   — — — — — — — —

6. having no end   — — — — — — —

7. state of being dim   — — — — — — —

8. a spoken sentence   — — — — — — — — —

9. state of being fat   — — — — — — —

10. state of being light   — — — — — — — — —

Now look at the letters in the black box. If you got all the answers right, those letters will make another word. This word means "the group that rules, or governs, a country." What is the word?

— — — — — — — — —

Phonics Home Activity: Ask your child to circle the suffix that appears at the end of each answer word. Then have your child either write a sentence using each word or give an example, such as *lightness:* feather.

Circle the word that will make each sentence tell about the picture. Then write the word on the line and circle the suffix in it.

leaf<u>less</u>   dark<u>ness</u>   ship<u>ment</u>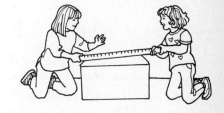

1. We will take a careful *measure(ment)*

   wireless   (measurement)   closeness

2. Jim is small, but he is quick and _____.

   fearless   sadness   encouragement

3. This is very good _____!

   breathless   readiness   entertainment

4. This broken umbrella is _____.

   worthless   stillness   improvement

5. She uses great _____ when she touches Spot's leg.

   careless   gentleness   development

Name _____

Read this story. Decide which word in the box belongs in each space. Then write the word in the space.

fearless	careless	announcement	encouragement
darkness	sadness	hopeless	appointment

Mark and John liked to solve mysteries. So they were happy when Mrs. Twimble made an *appointment* to see them one afternoon.

"My favorite gold pin is missing, boys," she said. "I'm so sad that I lost it!"

Mrs. Twimble's _____ made the boys sorry for her. "Don't worry," John said. "This case is not _____ at all. We'll find your pin!"

They looked through Mrs. Twimble's house, which was dark, lit by only a few lamps. Mark found the _____ scary. John wasn't scared, though. He tried to give Mark some _____.

"Stop shaking, Mark," he said. "Try to be _____ and forget about the dark." But Mark shook so hard that he knocked over a table.

"Oh, no! I'm so _____!" he said. Then he saw something small and bright on the floor by the table. "Shine the flashlight here, John!" he said.

They ran to find Mrs. Twimble. "We have a happy _____ to make," Mark said. "We have found your gold pin!"

Read the two words at the top of each box. Then
write the word that would come in between the
two words alphabetically.

1. **clutch — frog** elbow ghost brag *elbow*	**2.** **hurry — kitchen** fetch itch monkey _____	**3.** **nasty — quick** muscle range prance _____	**4.** **touch — watch** smart van yard _____
5. **block — branch** boil balloon bubble _____	**6.** **desert — door** daisy drift dimple _____	**7.** **plant — price** pinch poetry punish _____	**8.** **short — snarl** slither senior sparkle _____
9. **address — admit** adapt adjective adverb _____	**10.** **exit — extent** expose excess exact _____	**11.** **infect — insect** include injure into _____	**12.** **thick — thread** thorn thyme thaw _____

Name _____

Fill in the circle next to the word that would go in the blank if the words were listed alphabetically.

★ assure   banish   _____   diet
  ● crowd   ○ force   ○ every

1. inside   kilt   neon   _____
   ○ locker   ○ hornet   ○ phrase

2. magnet   _____   minute
   ○ message   ○ mortar   ○ mulch

3. school   scrape   _____
   ○ scallop   ○ scurry   ○ scoop

4. _____   velvet   waffle   yoke
   ○ zebra   ○ young   ○ uproar

5. topic   _____   tumble
   ○ trusty   ○ twinkle   ○ title

6. puffy   puncture   _____
   ○ pulley   ○ pumpkin   ○ puppet

7. likeness   match   parachute   _____
   ○ original   ○ needle   ○ quality

8. circle   _____   cradle
   ○ contrast   ○ chuckle   ○ cute

9. _____   gem   general
   ○ geometry   ○ gear   ○ gesture

Number right _____

Phonics Home Activity: Ask your child to read each completed list. Then help your child make a list of things in his or her room and put the list in alphabetical order.

Read the sentence. Decide how the underlined word should be divided into syllables. Write the letter of your answer on the line.

A   1. The zipper on my coat is stuck.

    A zip/per   B zi/pper   C zipp/er

_____ 2. We may all be able to travel to the moon in the future.

    A fu/tu/re   B fu/ture   C fut/ure

_____ 3. Mrs. Lewis bought chicken and ham at the market.

    A ma/rket   B mark/et   C mar/ket

_____ 4. A green parrot flew out of the tree.

    A parr/ot   B pa/rrot   C par/rot

_____ 5. It was very late when the plane finally arrived.

    A fi/nal/ly   B fin/al/ly   C fin/ally

_____ 6. Sam won first prize in the science contest.

    A con/test   B co/ntest   C cont/est

_____ 7. Describe your trip and don't leave out any details.

    A de/ta/ils   B det/ails   C de/tails

_____ 8. I had a very pleasant time on my vacation.

    A pleas/ant   B ple/as/ant   C plea/sant

_____ 9. Kay collects stamps from all over the world.

    A coll/ects   B co/llects   C col/lects

_____ 10. Sara set up a lemonade stand in front of her house.

    A le/mon/ade   B lem/on/ade   C lemo/na/de

Name _____

review

Read each meaning clue. Decide which word in the box goes with the meaning. Divide the word into syllables as you write it on the line.

humor	forward	pilot	closet	narrow
flavor	shadow	pillow	expert	journey

1. a person who has great skill in a special area

ex/pert

2. the taste of something

_____

3. not wide

_____

4. a place to keep clothes

_____

5. made when light is blocked

_____

6. travel from one place to another

_____

7. what makes something funny

_____

8. a soft bag used under a person's head during sleep

_____

9. going toward the front

_____

10. a person who flies a plane

_____

Phonics Home Activity: Ask your child to read each definition and the answer he or she wrote on the line. Then ask your child to try to use each word in a sentence.

Say each picture name. Read the words. Then fill in the circle next to the word that is divided into syllables correctly.

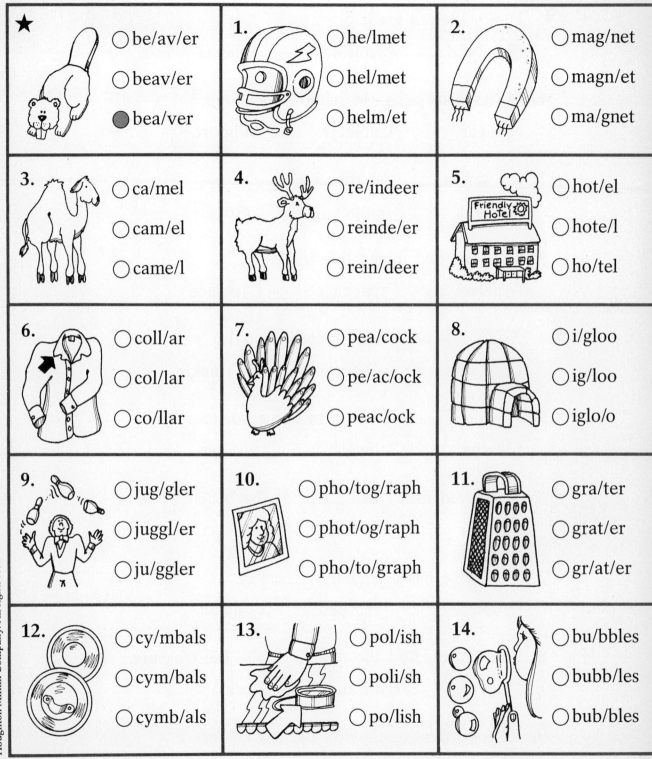

★
○ be/av/er
○ beav/er
● bea/ver

1.
○ he/lmet
○ hel/met
○ helm/et

2.
○ mag/net
○ magn/et
○ ma/gnet

3.
○ ca/mel
○ cam/el
○ came/l

4.
○ re/indeer
○ reinde/er
○ rein/deer

5.
○ hot/el
○ hote/l
○ ho/tel

6.
○ coll/ar
○ col/lar
○ co/llar

7.
○ pea/cock
○ pe/ac/ock
○ peac/ock

8.
○ i/gloo
○ ig/loo
○ iglo/o

9.
○ jug/gler
○ juggl/er
○ ju/ggler

10.
○ pho/tog/raph
○ phot/og/raph
○ pho/to/graph

11.
○ gra/ter
○ grat/er
○ gr/at/er

12.
○ cy/mbals
○ cym/bals
○ cymb/als

13.
○ pol/ish
○ poli/sh
○ po/lish

14.
○ bu/bbles
○ bubb/les
○ bub/bles

©

Number right _____

Name _____

135

Read each sentence and each group of words. Then fill in the circle next to the word that completes each sentence.

★ Henry blew a great big _____.

  ● bubble   ○ blister   ○ bucket

1. My favorite _____ in school is spelling.

  ○ sugar   ○ subject   ○ support

2. We saw a _____ at the zoo.

  ○ zebra   ○ zipper   ○ zero

3. The king and queen live in the _____.

  ○ parrot   ○ package   ○ palace

4. A _____ is a sea bird that cannot fly.

  ○ perfume   ○ penguin   ○ pickle

5. Grandma planted _____ in her garden.

  ○ tulips   ○ towels   ○ turkeys

6. We stayed in a small _____ at the beach.

  ○ collar   ○ cottage   ○ collect

7. This story has a friendly _____.

  ○ dragon   ○ darken   ○ detail

8. The pirates used the map to _____ the treasure.

  ○ locker   ○ locate   ○ local

9. Ed took this _____ with his new camera.

  ○ phonograph   ○ paragraph   ○ photograph

Number right _____

136 **Phonics Home Activity:** Ask your child to read the completed sentences. Then have your child choose two of the sentences to copy and illustrate on a separate piece of paper.

Circle the compound word that names the picture. Write the word on the line. Then circle the two base words in the word.

1.
backstop
barefoot
(backpack)

(back) pack

2.
headlight
headroom
headstand

_____

3.
workshop
workbench
workbook

_____

4.
seashell
eggshell
nutshell

_____

5.
snowball
snowshoe
snowfall

_____

6.
teamwork
teapot
teaspoon

_____

7.
horseshoe
hourglass
housewife

_____

8.
skylight
moonlight
flashlight

_____

9.
clothesline
underline
guideline

_____

10.
firefly
fireplace
firefighter

_____

11.
doorstep
doorway
doorknob

_____

12.
starfish
snapdragon
sandpaper

_____

Name _____

Read the two sentences next to each number. Write the word that completes the second sentence.

1. Kim is having a party.

She is _decorating_ the room.

decorated   decorating

---

2. Tony washed the windows.

Rita _____ the floor.

scrubbing   scrubbed

---

3. Mark wants to go for a ride.

He _____ the horse to the wagon.

hitches   hitching

---

4. Mrs. Parks comes home from a trip.

She _____ her suitcases into the house.

carrying   carries

Phonics Home Activity: Ask your child to read each pair of sentences and explain his or her word choices. Then have your child suggest sentences for the words that were not chosen.

Write the word that completes each sentence.

alive	incomplete	unpack	uncover	become
remove	dishonest	exchange	explain	return

1. Although no rain had fallen, the plants were still ___*alive*___.

2. The detective tried to _____ evidence of the crime.

3. A criminal is a _____ person.

4. The coat was too big so Mary wanted to _____ it.

5. He has worked hard to _____ a good doctor.

6. We will have to _____ the trees damaged in the storm.

7. I hate to _____ my suitcase after a vacation.

8. The repairs on the car are still _____.

9. Rosa will _____ what you have to do.

10. Will you _____ the book you borrowed after class?

A word that has a suffix in it is hiding in the letters beside each number. A clue to that word is given below the letters. Find the word and circle it. Then print the letters of the word in the boxes.

1. A D R I C H E S T L P
   the one with the most money

   `R` `I` `C` `H` `E` `S` `T`

2. X I C O L L E C T I O N L
   a group of things

3. S T A T E M E N T L G U Y R
   something said

4. R E L P Y E N D L E S S T Y
   goes on forever

5. G R N I N E T Y Y S N E S S
   one more than 89

6. S H O M A O N M E S S Y S T
   not neat

7. D A R K N E S S T Y A E L Y
   missing light

8. W R P A I N F U L T H E S S
   it hurts

9. G T O W M O N T H L Y E N T
   happening 12 times a year

Phonics Home Activity: Ask your child to read each word that he or she wrote in the boxes. Then ask your child to try to use each of the words in a sentence.

Say each picture name. Fill in the circle next to the
word that names or tells about the picture.

check

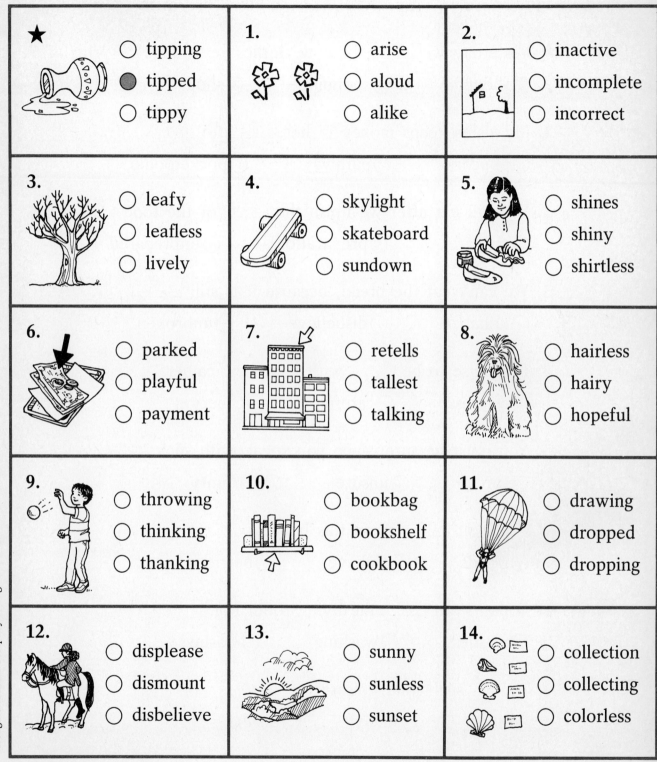

★
○ tipping
● tipped
○ tippy

1.
○ arise
○ aloud
○ alike

2.
○ inactive
○ incomplete
○ incorrect

3.
○ leafy
○ leafless
○ lively

4.
○ skylight
○ skateboard
○ sundown

5.
○ shines
○ shiny
○ shirtless

6.
○ parked
○ playful
○ payment

7.
○ retells
○ tallest
○ talking

8.
○ hairless
○ hairy
○ hopeful

9.
○ throwing
○ thinking
○ thanking

10.
○ bookbag
○ bookshelf
○ cookbook

11.
○ drawing
○ dropped
○ dropping

12.
○ displease
○ dismount
○ disbelieve

13.
○ sunny
○ sunless
○ sunset

14.
○ collection
○ collecting
○ colorless

©

Number right _____

Name _____ 141

Fill in the circle next to the word that completes each sentence.

★ Yesterday we _____ for new clothes.
   ● shopped   ○ shopping   ○ shops

1. My sister keeps money in her _____.
   ○ popcorn   ○ pathway   ○ pocketbook

2. We will eat after we finish the _____ of the food.
   ○ prepares   ○ preparation   ○ unprepared

3. We can't eat the bread, because it is still _____.
   ○ unbaked   ○ disbelieve   ○ unbroken

4. I promise to be _____ with your new camera.
   ○ careless   ○ careful   ○ cheery

5. You must be sure, since you speak with such _____.
   ○ surest   ○ unsure   ○ certainty

6. Come sit _____ us on this bench.
   ○ beside   ○ behave   ○ befriend

7. Today I am _____ the living room rug.
   ○ washes   ○ washing   ○ washed

8. I _____ such loud noises!
   ○ likes   ○ likely   ○ dislike

Number right _____ ©

Phonics Home Activity: Ask your child to read the sentences that he or she has completed. Then have your child circle any words that contain either a prefix or a suffix.

HOUGHTON MIFFLIN **Phonics** BOOK 5

Skills I Am Learning

Skill												
Short Vowel Sounds	1	2	3	4	5	6	7	8	9	10	**11**	**12**
Long Vowel Sounds	13	14	15	16	17	18	19	20	21	22	**23**	**24**
Short and Long Vowel Sounds	25	26	27	28	29	30	31	32	33	34		
ie, oo, ow	35	36	37	38	39	40	**41**	**42**				
ai, ay, oi, oy, oa, ew, ea	43	44	45	46	47	48	49	50	51	52	**53**	**54**
y as a vowel	55	56										
ind, ight	57	58										
Vowel plus r and re	59	60	61	62	**63**	**64**						
Clusters with r, l, s; three-letter clusters	65	66	67	68	69	70	71	72	**73**	**74**		
qu, squ, ng, nk, kn, wr	75	76	77	78	79	80						
Digraphs	81	82	83	84	**85**	**86**						
Alphabetical Order	87	88	89	90	91	92						
Syllables	93	94										
Generalization 1	95	96	97	98								
Generalization 2	99	100	101	102								
Compound Words	103	104	105	106								
Inflected Forms	107	108	109	110								
Prefixes **un, re, in, dis**	111	112	113	114								
Prefixes **a, be, ex**	115	116	117	118								
Suffixes **ful, ly**	119	120	121	122								
Suffixes **est, tion, ty**	123	124	125	126								
Suffixes **less, ness, ment**	127	128	129	130								
Review	131	**132**	133	134	**135**	**136**	137	138	139	140	**141**	**142**

Name _____

★**The numbers on the chart are workbook page numbers.**
   Light numbers are practice pages.
   Dark numbers are Check pages.